Hidden KNOWLEDGE

THOUGHTS *on the* AMERICAN PRESIDENCY

DR. OSCAR MCKINLEY

iUniverse

HIDDEN KNOWLEDGE
THOUGHTS ON THE AMERICAN PRESIDENCY

iUniverse books may be ordered through booksellers or by contacting:

iUniverse
1663 Liberty Drive
Bloomington, IN 47403
www.iuniverse.com
1-800-Authors (1-800-288-4677)

ISBN: 978-1-5320-5069-5 (sc)
ISBN: 978-1-5320-5070-1 (hc)
ISBN: 978-1-5320-5056-5 (e)

Library of Congress Control Number: 2018906629

Print information available on the last page.

iUniverse rev. date: 06/04/2018

CONTENTS

INTRODUCTION

was born in a small country town, in a two-room shack on the Mississippi Delta, on a hot September morning, right before dawn. It was a place called Doddsville, a one-horse town. It was in the fifties, and in those days the delivery doctor was called a midwife. I was told one day, when I was five years old and was being disobedient to my mother, about how she'd struggled bring me into this world. She explained to me that I'd weighed ten pounds. I think she told me that to see what kind of a reaction she would get. I paid no mind to what she said—it went in one ear and out the other—but somehow the words stuck with me. She also stated that the midwife who'd delivered me made a statement about never witnessing a baby with such strong lungs. She explained that I'd screamed like a baby wanting air-conditioning because it was too hot.

I was a hyper kid full of energy who made mistake after mistake. I think I got into trouble a lot because I learned fast as a baby, or maybe I was a little too curious. I had a sister nine years older. She made a habit of spanking me, which was something I hated. But the good thing about the spankings was that they only took place part-time because she went away for part of the year to spend time with her father. I also had a brother who was a year older than I was, and I adored him. I was younger but had the job of watching over him. The house that we lived in had holes in the walls, and the roof leaked. It was an old shack that probably was used by people during slavery, or it was built right after the Civil War. The house was on a plantation, off the road in a wooded area. I lived there for four years. The reason we moved was because I was on my death bed.

One day I was playing with my mother's friend's son, who was two years older than I was, and he played a lot rougher than I was used to. I was inside this small doghouse when he slammed the door on my head. The danger was that the door had rusty nails in it, and one went deep into my head. My mother grabbed me, ran to the plantation owner, and asked for his permission to take me to the doctor because she didn't have any money, and because it was usually the plantation owner who paid the doctor bills and charged the people later. But he said that I wasn't old enough to work, and so he could not spend money on me. My mother started screaming and took me home. That's how I got to be on my death bed. She took on the task of being my doctor, and I somehow got better. She later told me that I was talking out of my head and had a fever so high until my entire body was burning. But God smiled on me and healed my body.

Afterward, we moved fifty miles away and went to stay with my great, great grandparents. My grandmother was the daughter of a slave. The strange thing about it was that this slave was still alive, but she was very old and sat in a wheelchair. I was afraid of her, and she was so mean and loud, whereas my mother was a very kind, quiet lady who was shy at time. My grandmother had a problem reading and writing. One day she finally came out and told us the reason why she didn't go to school: she was afraid that some white man would kidnap or rape her. The walk to school was three miles from home. She would go hide all day and pretend that she'd gone to school.

MEETING MY DAD

was four years old the first time I laid eyes on my dad. At first I thought he was a white man, and I was reluctant to talk to him. But he proved to be a nice man and a well-deserved stepdad. I loved him with all my heart, and I know he loved me. He was an upper-middle-class black man in Mississippi. He had money in the bank, owned a nice house, and wrote checks for anything he needed. He was the guy whom most women wanted, but somehow my mother ended up with him—lucky break. It was like my life had just begun.

I forgot about all the past suffering, and so did my family. He took us under his wing, and I felt safe and protected at all times. He was a man among men. He always spoke softly and had a smile on his face. But I knew he was tough, and I wanted to be like him. I liked his style and his confidence, which never wavered. He would always tell me stories that provoked thoughts. One in particular was about this white doctor who treated all people the same, no matter what race or walk of life they came from. I knew then that one day I would become a doctor. I never did ask him who that doctor was, but looking back over the things he said, I think that doctor may have been his father.

My dad never really came right out and said what to do or what not to do. He left it up to us to make wise decisions. I remember him saying that God did not give the spirit of fear. (Great, now my imagination can run wild!) But there was one thing that I noticed in Mississippi that troubled me: black and white people feared each other. My mother was afraid of whites, but my dad wasn't. I sort of understood what Dr. Martin Luther King meant when he said, "I'm fearing no man, my eyes have seen the glory of the coming of the Lord." To me, it's a sin to be fearful because God did not give that spirit. I know fear comes and goes in all our lives, but one must not be controlled by fear. I hated the way people lived under the umbrella of fear in Mississippi, both black and white. I know now the dangers, but my daddy sheltered me from that danger. Most black people in Mississippi developed personalities through fear, but I wanted no part of that because I wasn't struggling with fear of the whites. I was free to think and free to become whoever God chose me to be. I was different and would not conform to their lifestyle. I essentially saw most people in Mississippi as racially insensitive buffoons, as beleaguered, distant, reprehensible creatures. This was a feeling that I hated myself for having to entertain. I still sometimes feel bad because of those inexplicable thoughts. But if I had yielded to their way of life, I would not be setting here today. So thanks, Dad, for letting me make those decisions without you questioning me.

Dr. Oscar McKinley

THE CHURCH HOUSE

I was raised in a Christian home and taught to love everyone and respect all adults. The one thing that would always upset my mother was not going to church. We went to church no matter what. The church was a pillar of the community, and kids were taught about Christianity at an early age. My mother was an usher, and my grandmother sang in the choir. Between my brother and little sister were stair steps, and we were about one year apart. Now, church was a place where kids could easily get into trouble. Because all the adults were usually keeping an eye on every move we made, it never seemed to fail that I always got into trouble for talking. I loved church and all the Christmas and Easter speeches they gave me, but I never learned my lines. When it was my turn to say my speech, I would start out but then act like, "Wow, I just forgot it." They would always laugh and pass me by; better luck next year. It was a game to me to see how many years could pass without them noticing.

I was responsible because I had a job when I was eight years old at church, cutting the grass in the graveyard. All of the other kids were afraid to do it, and so I capitalized on the deal and got extra money. The lady in charge of maintenance was also the person in charge of the church activities. She owned a restaurant, and I ate for free (another burger, please). I had a friend who sometimes helped me cut the grass. That friend happened to be bisexual, but I didn't care; he never acted oddly around me. I was simply glad there were others around who were different. I respected his difference.

During that time, the most popular game for kids was shooting marbles. We grew up shooting marbles almost every day. I always ended up buying more marbles, because I could never beat this guy; it was highway robbery. He would even go with me to pick out the new marbles. That was sort of strange, because I felt like I was actually buying the marbles for him. But he respected me, and at times he would say things like, "I wish you were my brother." I felt like I was his brother, and I used to protect him as I did my own brother. Those guys wouldn't hit back when picked on, and so I got into fights for them. My mother even kept my brother out of school a whole year, waiting on me to start school so I could protect him. We started school in the same grade. I was five and he was seven, but I turned six later that year. I wasn't perfect, and I used to give all my lunch money to kids who were hungry; I would go without lunch day after day, until my mother found out. She would give my lunch money to my brother, and he would give it to me at lunchtime.

I hated school from first grade through twelfth. I hated that some kids could eat and some couldn't. Plus, I didn't like being judged on how much I knew. Sometimes I would know the answer and wouldn't write or say it; that part was strange. I simply didn't need that kind of attention from people who would let little kids starve all day. One thing was good about school: I made lots of friends, even though I knew some of the kids because they went to my church. We stuck together like fingers in a glove. When most of us turned twelve years of age, we all got on what was called the morning bench. That was when one seeks one salvation. The adults explained that we needed to see a sign from God. It was something that I never understood or saw, however it did keep me alert and vigilant. I got baptized along with my friends in a huge creek. It was beautiful. All the ushers and mothers wore white, and the kids had on long white robes.

COMPUTER POLITICIAN

t always seemed to happened right before I was ready to write. I felt a deep sorrow, as if the world was closing in on me, and writing was the only way to escape the pain. It was the antidote to solving the misery plaguing my soul. I wrote no matter the time of day or night. I felt a moral obligation to share all the books I had read and the knowledge I had accumulated throughout the years. It all seemed fresh in my mind, ready to explode on to paper. There were times I felt like the Democratic Party had a hunger for my writings. I could make a statement or recommend a thing, the media would catch it, and it was off to the races in a hurry, often that same day. It was a super connection with the media. I learned early that there were people depending on me to deliver certain things and make certain things happen. It kept me on my toes, because in some strange way I felt like I was doing a reality show without a paycheck. But my writings actually felt like a show that was filled with book knowledge, street sense, God's wisdom, and supernatural powers. That part is unexplained. It was like I was teaching American history and God's word, and exposing the evil that pledged our nation as well as the world. The intense level at times was maxed out trying to stay focused on the American people instead of my own feelings. But I made sure my writings were not misguiding people with any misinformation; it was like the media and I had a connection that was solid like a rock. I was one of the main sources getting out information. At times it was scary, because I knew the law makers just might move on my recommendations. Altogether, it pressured me to study long and hard before writing anything of significant value. I didn't hold back, and it was like ripping through a cold bologna sandwich with a can of black-eyed peas. I wrote with confidence like a king sitting on his throne, but no one in public ever recognized me. No paparazzi—wow, what a life. I knew I could make headlines at any given time, and no one knew it was me. This was splendid.

I stumbled into writing with just two people in mind, and yes, the pen is mightier than the voice; trust me on that. I write at least two to three times per week. It's all basically creative writing. It started to take shape in my mind because I was tired of the way people were painting pictures of President Obama. God kept telling me to write, and I kept telling God that no one would listen. One day, God reminded me of one of my old college professor who'd explained to me that I was a comedian and needed to find a way to use it. I smiled at him but kept pursuing my education. Deep in my heart, I knew he was right. Well, my first mission came into play. I realized that I had to rescue President Obama and reiterate his greatness. It placed him in the twelfth spot among the best presidents. God kept saying, "Do more." This president was heavy on my mind. I didn't know where or how to keep going until God spoke to me again. He said, "You're funny, so use what I have given you. Just cut loose, Oscar."

My first writings were about great men who advanced the rights of colored people. It took off, but I still hadn't made the connections with the comedy aspect. I waited a while, but there was something inside of me that was persistent and kept pushing me to write truths along with comedy. One day, I decided to inject comedy along with my truths into my writing. The Republican Party candidate, Donald Trump, was running for president, but to me he was a crazy con man straight out of a comic book. Why not write about this guy over time and expose his frailties to the American people? I began to write short stories about issues as they arose, and I combined them with politics, always using comedy. The main thing that separated me from other writers was my storytelling and of course my laugh-out-loud ability—my signature moves. To make it plain and simple, I'm the LOL guy.

I decided to share my short stories in the form of a book. They are mainly about incidents that happened before the presidential election of

2016, as well as after the election about the new president's behavior and how he was handling his new job—or shall I say, *trying* to handle it. Along the way, my writings and videos gave me an opportunity to single-handedly saved Obama's health care. I did it from my computer at my home. I also gave a huge boost, encouraging women to evolve like a Pokémon (the Me Too movement). I'm not sure how much credit I should get for the Alabama senate race, but I worked on that one. There were also times that I influenced powerful lawmakers whenever needed, but only for the betterment of mankind. At no times did I abuse my powers. I tested it a couple of times and found out that I was capable of influencing other world leaders, especially the pope. But I would always back off when people began to notice how powerful I was.

I think my education really came in handy. I hold a double doctorate in special education and psychology, with a degree in religion. There were lots of people who knew what I was doing and warned me to not take the lead, but I was already one of the most powerful people on the planet who was not a president. One might say that I was the leader of the Democratic Party. It was strange being that powerful, and you know you're among the greats because you're doing the impossible. What a trip—just me and my computer. I started out with an old computer that was broken on most days. But eventually I got one of the best, and it helped put my foot down on my writings for the betterment of the world. I always knew that it wasn't about me. It was entirely about the American people. I'm probably the world's greatest philosopher and politician without a title. I went to hell and back dealing with the devil over the last two years. But now I know that my writings helped change America and certain parts of the world. I did it all through these writings in my book.

The Writings That Dominated Politics for Over a Year

BEFORE THE END

This perilous spectacle insinuates a strange love affair between Donald Trump and Vladimir Putin, which surpasses Romeo and Juliet. They keep jumping in and out of bed and messing with Americans' heads. I think they see exquisite beauty in each other. It's a two-way love affair that cannot be denied, and it's a very tight squeeze. Oh, yeah, believe me, it's sweeter than honey. Roses are red and violets are blue. They love each other, and not me and you. This relationship does not include the American people, which makes it very dangerous. Like the Beverly Hillbillies TV show: oil, that is—black gold, Texas tea. The question is whether this guy is capable of leading the free world—or for that fact, his own businesses. I think not because of his personal problems, not able to focus. I hear people keep saying that Donald Trump needs to start listening. He's trying, but he's just not capable. His ears are trained to hear certain people or things.

As for the electoral college vote, I think you guys have seen and heard enough to vote out this guy (disqualifying the presidency). You will have done your job and protected this nation. Send it back to deadbeat congress, let them deal with this guy because they created him. So wash your hands and be free of this disaster. Congress wrestles with this kind of stuff all the time, nut balling. There has been too much interference from a foreign country that has rigged our election. Let congress deal with Donald Trump; it's cut-and-dried. Make sure you take away thirty-seven votes and sleep well, good people; just pass it on. Instead of Make America Great Again, concentrate on saving the Klan in Washington, DC. I'm sensing others are involved in this Russian scandal that's playing hide and seek. Around ten to fifteen double agents are still in this administration, along with the House of Representatives and the Senate, keeping their fingers crossed and hoping not to be exposed. They are considered Confederates and are connected to a foreign country. Listen to how they talk, as if this colluding with a foreign country and conspiracy means nothing. They are parading as Americans but really are not. They are Confederate intruders, trying to overthrow our government. They have betrayed the American people in one of the worst ways possible by colluding with a foreign government.

It's just a matter of time before they start ratting out each other, because they will hand over the big cheese. It's amazing how fast these people are willing to sell out America, because they don't like the rainbow country that we are. Most of us love America and want to see America great again— the way President Obama left it. But telecommunications with a nonsense approach are all this administration has to offer, and it's all *Mission Impossible,* or sort of like *Dumb and Dumber.* Now, it's gloomy and dull as a witch without her broom, but this is no witch hunt—give her the broom. Our song "I Feel Good" by James Brown is fake news. Donald Trump has been quarterbacking and doing well enough to deflect the crowd by using his faking techniques, hiding the ball. He did it so well that most people couldn't really tell where the ball was. But now, the referee has thrown a flag on the play, and the team is going to get penalized. They're calling it back. The call is illegal procedure.

FOOL'S GOLD

*D*onald Trump simply wants some respect. We have to understand that part, because he has a damaged ego. He has been scrutinized, and attempts have been made to disqualify him as president. But isn't he the rock and savior of America who, as he put it, is "gonna sanctify America"? He has put America at his feet while evolving from Super Fly to Superman. His movements are quick, faster than a rattle snake. But there is still this one thing that can bring him to a halt and stop him in his tracks, his kryptonite, and that is his taxes. He has been beating his opponent with the kitchen sink while holding hands with the foreign leader and dancing with the old speaker. He's a cool cat.

Surprise—we will have to see your taxes now, Superman, or that title will have to go, because it's too serious to not know your finances. The news channels have continually requested his taxes. Donald Trump simply tells them to get lost because he's doing his thing. He must be thinking that we are a country of fools, but he shouldn't get near the house without showing us his taxes. It's time to get real and let up on Hillary Clinton, because this guy isn't real. There has to be a way to force this guy to show his taxes. We have to protect our country. The American people deserve the right to see his taxes. That is what we do as Americans: get to the bottom of things. He could turn out to be the joke.

WRONG COUNTRY

*D*onald Trump seems to be a likable guy, but there's a problem: he lies constantly. He leaves most Americans thinking that he's the type of guy who wants a gun in one hand and the Confederate flag in the other, and there is no middle ground. Most of his followers don't like black people and seem to be filled with hate. They make derogatory statements about the previous president on race alone, and they never gave him a chance. The Confederate States have voted for the Republican candidate for years, but they are not the party of Lincoln anymore. They switched from being Democrats to Republicans right after the Civil Rights Bill was signed by a Democratic president (that's a clue). I think they still hate Lincoln.

It is unclear to me if they honor the Confederate flag more than the United States flag. Maybe they still want to overthrow the US government. These people are monsters and are filled with hate. I'm sure they know that Donald Trump is insane by now, but I think they see an opportunity here to rise up against the government. Donald Trump is their leader, and it doesn't make a difference if he's right or wrong. I have been under the impression that she stood for something positive. How low are these people willing to go? It's scary, because Donald Trump is insane.

HOG SLOP

ow can anyone be so deceived and buy that con game that Donald Trump and Vladimir Putin just ran? People, this was all planned. Because Donald Trump doesn't make humanitarian decisions in that manner; wealth has to be involved. Plus, helping those people goes against his philosophy as a white nationalist, and that's something he holds dearly. He will go to any extreme to divert attention, even war. Remember what he tweeted to the previous president about war in the Middle East? All of that doesn't participate in any part of it. (Evidently, it was hogwash.) This chain of events was done in steps—the con begins.

First Secretary Tillerson made a statement to set it up. America will no longer be after the Middle East's President Assad for war crimes. Then all of a certain, Assad stupidly uses poison gas. That's too stupid to believe. Then impulsive Donald Trump reacts; tell it to the birds. It happens too fast, and the communications were too far from normal behavior. It's the way impulsive Donald Trump operates: plan one second, then react the next. Now, in order for this con to work, the United States must lift Russia sanctions—give Russia something. America now needs Russia (not true).

Okay, now, the con is supposed to be set up, so Secretary Tillerson goes to Russia to make a deal with Russia. (Why do we need a fake deal with fake people?) This con is about lifting the sanctions. Check this out: do you really think a man who will take away insurance from the elderly and babies in this country cares about the babies in Syria? Donald Trump was ready to repeal Obamacare without reading it—heartless. Just another act of deception, which is all he's about, a thug act.

Tillerson and Donald Trump think the American people are stupid and incapable of brainstorming the facts (whitewash). Russia is playing along and talking tough, but, nothing will happen because it's the big con (lift sanctions). Wake up, people. Understand that it's still Donald Trump. Remember, he's incapable of change. It's a game to him, and he's not with us.

FINALLY UNITED

*A*merican Indians live on reservations, and most blacks live trapped in the inner cities. It's understood how they got there; however, they have contributed many great things to America, and a lot of them live comfortably within the American system. They have a clear picture of someone like "the Sexy Guy" being the oppressor. No way would any of these groups vote this guy into the presidency. Confusion is still taking place, and there was one that was on the Civil Rights Bill that was added at the last minute. They didn't do anything to be on the bill; in fact, it's unclear if they are aware of even being on the Civil Rights Bill. It's under sex, which brings the American white woman aboard the bill.

I'm writing this in hopes of her understanding how she moved from secretarial to powerhouse jobs. It's the law that rode on the backs of poor, mostly uneducated blacks who marched and died to make progress in America. I can't comprehend how 53 percent of American women voted against the struggle. I think without the Civil Rights Movement, she would still be in the kitchen. It's a joy to see her marching for rights these days. Finally, we might move forward and prevent another Sexy Guy from the presidency.

PEOPLE, GET READY

t takes skill to deal off the bottom of the deck—and a lot of nerve. We all know it's called cheating. But it's very rewarding for a presidential crook. You get tired of winning because it's impossible to lose. I used to love to watch the television show *Maverick*. It was a western about a gambler who cheated at cards. He always left town in a hurry, usually because of people chasing him. People shouldn't get rewarded for being dishonest; at least, that's what we were taught, as well as to never lie, but it's a new day now.

However, the heat is on. Our song is "It's Gonna Be a Showdown" by the Rance Allen Group. Now, con artists usually grab and leave because it's foolish to stick around; you might get caught. Did somebody try to fool us and say that we would get tired of winning? Probably it's just another con. It's Flip Wilson's ego. Try watching Flip Wilson on *The Dean Martin Show*. Well, we as a nation now understand racism and the suffering it projects onto people of color. I think we are on our way finally to becoming one nation under God. Our song is "People, Get Ready" by the Impressions.

THE GOLDEN VOICE

One president has given us a new birth. In so many different ways, we Americans are travelling through time with President Obama. Over an eight-year period, it can somehow be equated to a ride on the Starship *Enterprise* that's going places no one has ever been before. It has been remarkable with astonishing grace. No one on earth can be a greater president than Obama. Only Jesus has changed the world as he did. This president's greatness will be talked about for thousands of years. He has put in motion the course to deliver the people from bondage worldwide. We won't turn back.

THE GODFATHER OF POLITICS

*P*resident Obama gave his greatest speech tonight. It appears that he took greatness to another level. While he spoke, the entire nation was calm, because he calms us, takes the stress off of us, and puts it on his shoulders. He's a real man, not a crybaby (Donald wants his bottle). As I sat there listening to President Obama, I tried to figure out how in the world someone could ever reach his level on earth, because there is no one in his class. This man has to be an angel sent directly from heaven. The Bible says that there will be angels among us, and we have seen one tonight. Long live the greatest world leader of all time, including all the pharaohs, kings, queens, and American presidents. President Obama tops them all. God wanted him black for a reason. He makes us proud to be black. Well, it's here now. James Brown said, "Say it loud: I'm black and I'm proud."

BABY SETTING

*M*ost Americans are caught up in a baby setting—a very confused, hallucinating, exaggerating, nut balling Bozo the Clown. The question is who's changing the diaper next. Schizophrenia is a disease that is very dangerous, and most people suffering from this disease may see or hear things that are not real. They don't comprehend the norm. They live in constant fear, and it's vigorously debilitating over time. It's preposterous to think these people will get better, so wake up, everybody. Donald Trump's fabricated world is magnified with sick people playing his game—progress only for the wealthy. He's always talking negatively, projecting onto someone else, and pointing his finger that it's their fault; he never takes the blame. I can't imagine following a sick person like that who's monkeying around. That person is insinuating violence, maybe starting a race war. Everything is fine and that nut can't see it. Maybe it's because he's the nutcracker.

NEVER MAKE IT

I just finished listening to seven different presidents give speeches. One thing I learned: these guys were all smart and very intelligent, and they all were good speakers. But there were commonalities. They were all were loved and admired by the American people. These presidents were some of the greatest speakers of all times. I listen carefully to hear the difference in their messages. After listening closely, I have come to the conclusion that it was one voice speaking of unity and equality. Let me also add that Dr. Martin Luther King never became president, but he should have.

When I look at Donald Trump, I see a fisherman or a logger, not a president. Now, there's nothing wrong with fishermen or loggers. Donald Trump shouldn't be able to walk the halls where these great men roamed. He's an illegitimate president, and that's why he's struggling all the time. He's always involving the American people with created madness, with one revelation after another—and it keeps getting worse. He's really losing his mind; it's like a toddler under pressure.

CRYING IN THE STREETS

I'm sure some of you have experienced buying a pair of new shoes, and somehow the salesperson accidentally puts the same foot shoe in the box, so you get stuck with two lefts or two rights. But you decide to wear them anyway. The shoes go with your outfit and makes you look so cute. You forgot about the excruciating pain of wearing two right shoes (reality sets in). You try to keep pace with your group, but it hurts too badly. Now, in life we change friends sometimes. They don't feel our pain, and they are too busy being macho men (let's cry together). We need to connect and share the burden while holding the line for America's health care, because we can't stop now. Always remember that God did not give the spirit of fear, and he's not afraid of the devil. I may not be able to be there, but I'm always near. You can move mountains if you can believe. Our song is "Ain't No Stopping Us Now" by McFadden and Whitehead.

SHARING AMERICA

eauty and the Beast is a movie that has left a good impression on me and my kids. The movie was about an old lady who came to a rich, young prince's castle in the middle of the night; she was cold and hungry and asked to come inside. He said no, and then she put a curse on him, turning him into a beast. Most of you probably have seen the movie or know the story. The trick was that a girl would have to fall in love with this creature within a certain period of time, in order to restore him to a normal person. It's interesting how the Beast was transformed into a wonderful, likable human being. The movie is relaxing and upbeat. The odds were against the Beast ever finding love, but he prevailed. In all honesty, he was ugly and scary with a bad attitude. He would bully everyone in the castle. He was that way for years, but finally a beautiful girl came to the castle one day and gave him hope. I really didn't want her close enough for him to grab her. But she didn't fear him, and she changed him into something likable even though he was still ugly. We begin to see a person emerging, the girl fell in love with the Beast, and the curse was lifted.

By those standards, looks doesn't matter and everyone has a chance. Yes, a lot of times we get hung up on appearance. We must ask ourselves just how important are looks. Do looks guide us through life? Do we make our decisions based on looks, or do we avoid anyone and anything that's unappealing to us? How does it look to see Indians in the shape they are in today, knowing America really belong to them? How does it look that blacks have worked three hundred years for free? How does it look that mostly whites have come to America within the last one hundred years? If your answer makes you angry, then you are not a part of America, because this is who we are. Go read the constitution: we're all equal. Who are you to override the constitution and feel you should have special privileges because of looks? That was a mistake made by a bunch of fools years ago.

Donald Trump has been tiptoeing around lately, trying to duck his mood swings, but he's still all about looks. He has been talking like a love bird undercover with a powerful lawman, as well as with hate group leaders. A new personality has emerged in Donald Trump that we have never seen before, and it's strange and impossible to be true. Donald Trump used to do the jump back Jack—see you later, alligator, right down to the funky Broadway. But now, all of a sudden he's civil? He thinks he has it made now.

Surprise—we fooled you and your mob squad. Blacks will come out to vote. We now see this election as forty acres and a mule, so let's get busy. That is what President Obama has asked us to do, and we still follow him. So go vote now. It's the great equalizer. Dr. Martin Luther King's dream is in play here, so we must carry it out and vote like never before.

Dr. Oscar McKinley

THE HOUSE OF HORROR

hy does the White House look and feel so wired these days, with blatant contradictions? We are wondering whether they are all genuinely Americans. It doesn't feel like a good place to go anymore because they are impervious to the truth. For some of us, maybe, it feels like a dream and living in a fairy tale—once upon a time in a faraway land that was ruled by vampires. Then again, it may feel like America has been stolen, infiltrated by a wicked force that's too sexy for his hair. You keep telling yourself that it will be all right and will soon be over. But the minute you hear that nagging voice, or read an insane tweet, PTSD shouts. Depression is a normal thing these days, so having a therapist and talking about it is a good thing.

Today we seen the previous president, and it all went away for a few. Wow, don't we trust him? President Obama was the greatest president of all time. I truly think there was only one leader in history similar to him, and it was Alexander the Great. No other leader comes close. He has set the tone for modern-day world leadership, and the world loves his style of leading. When this president was leading, those were the good old days, and America was great. Now it's complicated, and our song is "Ball of Confusion" by the Temptations.

HATE VERSUS LOVE

ate groups are victims of paranoid delusions, also called delusions of persecution. This diagnosis is attached to a person experiencing fear and anxiety. One may feel trapped and unable to make rational decisions. Usually this type of diagnosis brings about a lot of exaggerating. As an example, a person may think something is happening or going to happen, but it's a figment of one's imagination. It will never happen, but it creates tremendous stress and fear for these individuals. Many have lost touch with reality while holding fast to a nonsense delusion.

One must be careful because this disease can grow into full-blown schizophrenia, with no reciprocal relationship with the norm, leaving them at a loss for knowledge and becoming stagnated in ignorance. Also, they become embroiled in serious anger and hatred with selfish views, displaying an evil, maniacal behavior from the past. They have lost the art of versatility and can no longer brainstorm or understand a theory from facts—sort of like cartoon people with an angry orientation. They're trapped, still entertaining prehistoric ideals from the past, which is not good. Donald Trump needs to learn the reasons why people apologize. Our song today is "Stop in the Name of Love" by Diana Ross and the Supremes.

Tap Dancing President

f the America people can tolerate Donald Trump, the Sexy Guy, and still have the notion that America is a leading figure within the civilized world, that's an insane level of ignorance. The world isn't dumb. The Sexy Guy has signified that his genes are superior to others—just as Hitler claimed before he destroyed Germany. It appears that they are two ducks in a pond. We must watch carefully to not normalize this psychotic behavior, because it's demonic. One of the main problems is that it goes directly against everything the Bible teaches about being created equal. Superior genes mean that God lied about his creation. However, the Bible states that God cannot lie. So does that mean that white nationalism and hate groups are going against God?

I understand that Donald Trump went up to Capitol Hill, and put his foot down wearing a size five shoe, and he had on small gloves that didn't look normal. He slapped a few people around and threatened to run every congressman out of town who didn't vote for his bill, mafia style. Let's put it in layman's terms: as Richard Pryor said, "Get the hell out of here." He also explained in one of his interviews that he was smarter than Einstein. That I can believe—except, it would have to be the Einstein of the Neanderthals. Yeah, there are Republicans in congress who have been there for years, and to them Donald Trump is probably looking like a two-minute president: all in a nutshell and headed out the door.

THE GHETTO PRESIDENT

*T*here are certain behaviors that are attached to a person from the inner city, the ghetto. Please don't get me wrong on the word *ghetto*. I'm headed someplace with this. Have you ever noticed how most people from the inner city act? It's as though they are the coolest people in the world, and it's very important to them. They learn quickly how the game is played for real, and it's not acting like a movie. Learning ghetto behavior is common in America; most races went through this style of living, and they all responded the same: cool and in control. The embodiment of American culture, included gangsters, pimps, and hustlers—the people without.

But when people become educated, they sort of reform from that behavior. I'm sure most of us have met white people who wanted to act black, and vice versa. Donald Trump wants so badly to be a black man. He doesn't want anyone white to blow his cool. I think it's crazy cool and scary at the same time to have a ghetto president. One of the first things you learn is to not to bark too loudly, or, at the wrong person, because you don't want enemies. Funky mosquitoes spread diseases, and they like sucking on you and will drink you dry. No one really wants them around. Impeach!

The False Prophets

*O*n the one hand, the new administration keeps slipping further and further into the abyss of collusion and obstruction. Our song is "Little Lies" by Fleetwood Mac. On the other hand, people have a tendency to follow the ones with the biggest mouths. A foretelling story is someone who can see into the future and warn of coming events, which is exactly what a prophet does. But when prophets are wrong, they are considered to be false prophets. Hold on; I'm going to run back to the Old Testament again. Remember, that used to be the only way God sent his word, through prophets. But somewhere along the line, false prophets began surfacing. They were usually appointed by kings to fool the people. These fictitious appointees intensified divisions among the people. These false prophets always lied and never brought a message that benefited the poor.

God empowered his prophets to be able to do powerful things that would expose a false prophet. Let's be clear as day: a false prophet is a fake and lives off one lie to the next, just like discovering fool's gold. I have always pictured a false prophet as being able to speak like Chicken George in *Roots*. Remember him? He mesmerized people with his tone and character, even while he was still a slave. It came down to his chicken winning his freedom, but that chicken lost. I went walking alone that night, and I cried as if I were a slave seeking my freedom. The pain was excruciating, and depression set in for a couple of days. I was captivated with Chicken George. As a young kid, that slave was my hero for a while.

Donald Trump should only listen to wise counsel—people like Snapping Bulldog Harry, Sweet Cell Block Bubba, and old sour speaker of the house Newt Gingrich. They'll know what to do—probably smuggle him out of our country. Okay, the first thing should be moving him out of the hood, away from the White House that he lives in at the present. It's been a bad influence on Donald. Those crooked staffers inside have taken away all his toys. Sad. Let's rock our song "Good Golly, Miss Molly" by Little Richard, at Muhammad Ali's fiftieth birthday.

MONEY HONEY

he true cause of the president ranting is a writing called "Money Honey." This was written a day before the rant with the NFL. I'm positive it's a diversion—and no coincidence, he's distracting Americans along with the money printer in hopes of not printing the money, because it's at the bottom of the list for these white men. The speaker may have a say, because I think he understands the urgency for this nation to see more good.

Donald Trump says he's not a racist. Well, let's make some moves toward not discriminating and acting prejudice toward blacks. If you are not a racist, then you will see these blacks as deserving to be on American money. It would be no problem for you. I'm positive George W. Bush would print the money, and so would Ronald Reagan. We want Harriet Tubman on the twenty-dollar bill now. We are tired of looking at Jackson's ugly, bushy hair. That looks creepy. We want to see a beautiful black woman on that twenty. Can you get that done next week? You say you're not a racist, so that's a starting point—prove it. Also, the Obama Administration redesigned the backs of the five- and ten-dollar bills, displaying some great civil rights–era leaders and the different movements. But I do believe that Donald Trump will make excuses and block printing the money, because he wants only white men on money You are not a racist? Then prove it! From observing you, it appears that you are the definition of a racist, maybe the president of a hateful mob. Well, here's our song: "Chariots of Fire."

Dr. Oscar McKinley

CRAZY WORLD

*T*he Trump Administration takes the cake—essential for being the leading therapeutic institution in the world. They have made some theoretical, extraordinary advancements within the mental health field. Probably it's because they have the number one client in the world: Donald Trump. They have taken psychology to infinity and beyond. It would be preposterous to neglect to note how good they must be; the world is still here. They actually come face-to-face with the bogeyman on a daily basis. It looks like it's left up to someone within the administration to keep us safe. A shout-out to the administration: we need you to be our hero.

Please remember people that when you are talking to a person who may be suffering from impulse control, always talk calm and be relaxed while talking to him, because he sees everything in a hurry. Try telling him to think about things a while and get back with you later, and set a time. You have to teach Donald Trump how to solve problems. Because when he does not see his way out of stressful situations, he will revert to drastic measures. Keep a handle on him.

ROCKET MAN

I can't begin to fathom the damage a modern-day nuclear weapon can create. Just the thought of such a weapon with a magnitude of destruction that kills millions of people is frightening. But there is another nuke that the Republicans are overlooking, and it's call Obamacare. Removing the health care bill at this point in time is the same as signing a death sentence. Donald Trump, the loose cannon and rocket man, will fire off nukes and kill millions. First stop, nuclear weapon number one, which is Obamacare. It's in the process of a countdown. I'm still able to fight another man, but I won't fight babies, the elderly, the sick and defenseless people.

I have dedicated my life to God. God is saying to stand up and to not be weak. Remember, they tried to buy off Dr. Martin Luther King, but he said God was telling him to make the crooked roads straight and explained that he couldn't do that. Imagine if he had sold us out. There would be no women or blacks in the senate. It would still only be white males who rule America. Sometimes you have to walk alone, but that doesn't matter. God is with you now, and so who can be against you? The devil wants to destroy America, and only the strong will be left standing. Make sure it's you. The song for today is "Let's Stay Together" by Al Green.

HOSTAGE

*I*t has been amazing, even astonishing, watching Donald Trump. He's the most interesting man in the world. He knows every single thing that's going on, whether it's naughty or nice. I underestimated gray-headed American white men. I finally found out who the real Super Fly was, and he's not black. It's none other than Donald Trump. He's fascinating with his falsehoods and speaks his mind as if there aren't any consequence. He's above everyone else, like the Lone Ranger. He has demonstrated radiant power that would make any hate group step aside, because he's good evil. There is no pussyfooting around with this guy. His lewd remarks had better be okay with all Americans because he's holding us hostage. America's news women had better shut up and overlook his retardation, because he attacks women. Well, at least the news women are trying. It's the news men who are actually disappointing. They act as if they are afraid of Donald Trump.

I'm beginning to understand his wolf tickets, just like 40 percent of America who will vote for him. He's old school, and he knows how to keep white women and black people in line. It's funny how his boy Newt Gingrich, the old speaker, disrespects women in the same manner, displaying bad manners; it must be a club. Donald Trump stepped on the whole nation today by congratulating the old speaker on national television, which was unbelievable to witness. What is left for kids to think? Somebody has to stand up to this guy. The constitution is no longer secure. That's why deadbeat congress worked so hard at stopping President Obama's job bills. With no jobs, they control blacks and keep them in one place. They also do not believe in a woman becoming president, and they are working hard to stop Hillary Clinton. I felt sorry for the news lady today when she was literally attacked by the old ghetto players. I finally get it with these men. Women and blacks are in trouble and had better stay in their place, because these white men rule through putting fear into people. As for the Hispanics, he's going to get rid of you guys simply because you are not part of his plan. Only then will he feel that America will be great again. Remember that it's all about women being in their place, blacks in their place, and the Hispanics gone. That makes the white man reign supreme again. Sounds like bad luck for the rest of us.

FLOPPING

*D*onald Trump has been floating like a butterfly and stinging like a bee outside the ring. Pathetic. On top of that, Donald has gone from holding hands with a known dictator, Vladimir Putin, to making him a tight squeeze. The puzzle is almost completed with this foreign country, and the choir is ready to sing—a little too close. But it's possible that this love affair will be broken up by a smart president (someone who loves this country) and his administration. Now, Donald Trump has started dancing off the wall and living crazy, because that's the only way since the investigation started. Donald can't sleep these days, and he has been tossing and turning all night. I don't think this guy will ever be sworn in as president, simply because we don't know which country he represents; he could be just after oil. We can't take that chance. He's going to tweet and say that he's his own rock and roll fantasy, so please don't doubt it. He gets angry and reverts to undignified mannerisms. He's nuts.

Well, Americans can get lost now. Donald Trump doesn't need us anymore. He is only concerned about his feelings, and it stops there. He wants to divide America and start a race war. He hates blacks, Mexicans, and poor whites. This masquerade has to end—unless we are a country of showbiz. This man can never send our kids off to war with a reality show going on. Oh, yeah—he says that he loves wars. That alone should make us furious. It's unprecedented.

JUDAS

*L*istening to Donald Trump speak is like listening to an uneducated man rattling along—the lost, empty wagon syndrome. He uses broken English and slang language, almost ghetto. I'm sure Americans would be more receptive if Donald Trump simply used sign language. He's not capable of explaining himself, and that's why he has a cleanup crew—remember his mind readers? That's childish and dangerous, especially dealing with some Asian countries. I can't believe this guy is headed north to do a campaign rally. I always thought the South would welcome people like Donald, not the North. Are we surrounded? That makes this campaign even more difficult and confusing. It appears he's mocking us now by saying nasty things about certain races. This person is speaking for Americans—are we nuts? Donald Trump started out as a joke, but it's out of hand now. This guy is belligerent and a flat-out nut baller. But he is picking up steam.

THE LAST MAGIC TRICK

*P*aranormal, oratorical magic can be called tricks or possibly illusions. These tricks always appear to look impossible, like magic. The performers' act was called magic tricks. It has been said that Harry Houdini and David Copperfield were the best. That brings me to my point. Let's use storytelling as magic. I was raised in the South, and yeah, I still have nightmares from that cotton. Things were sort of crazy at times, but they were very rewarding because you had to understand another language. An example of this is equating a lie with telling a story. Most of the people deep in Dixie would never use the word *lie*; it was always referred to as telling a story.

So let's give Donald Trump a break. Let's give greatness where greatness is due, even if it's negative sometimes. Donald Trump is a great man in his own way (bootlegged). But he's speaking a language that most Americans aren't familiar with; it's foreign country. Donald Trump is president and it's the greatest trick of all time. I can't tell if he's going or coming; he's putting it to us. He fires generals and then praises them. I'm not sure if he remembers. Now, they say that they are the party of good hope. How in the world do we communicate with this party these days, except negotiating through a foreign country, Russia?

THE GOOD AND THE UGLY

onald Trump is placing his relatives throughout this administration. I'm wondering whether any of them will have any control over the nukes. If so, we are in more trouble than a whale without a tail. This sexy man's goal seems to be to humiliate every America who does not believe in white supremacy. Now, there were eighteen presidents who owned slaves. Andrew Jackson owned two hundred, and believe it or not, George Washington owned 317, yet he is listed as one of the greatest presidents. That's insanely stupid. In fact, there are a lot of presidents listed in the top ten who were slave owners, which is the embodiment of evil. So we accept slavery as a normal thing these days and continue to praise these guys who were guilty of those hideous crimes, which shows ignorance at its peak. That's what it appears to be.

Let's take an honest look at these people's actions, and that includes gruesome, monstrous, and oblivious acts time after time. These nutty presidents felt righteous about having slaves. They may have contributed to America along with the slaves, but there were absolutely nothing really good about these presidents who owned slaves, and they should not be spoken of so highly. That's why America is in the mess we are in among crazy people. I'm a passionate, tender, and affectionate guy who believes in love. I love to think about love. Simply pronouncing the word moves me. There's something about the sound that virtually puts it above every other word. The scriptures states that God is love. We are creatures that are created in God's own image. So love is the benefactor that inspires us to vigorously seek out significant others. It's tough being without love. I used to work with gang members back in the nineties, and believe it or not, those guys loved one another. They supported each other because they had learned to be a family. Yeah, groups band together for support.

I remember when I really tried living in the South, right after being in the military. Whites and blacks did not communicate at all there. It was too much for me because I had become accustomed to having white friends. I had gotten used to the laughter and the long conversations on a daily basis. It was too much to handle. I needed whites in my life. Somehow race seemed to balance things in America better for me. So, I left on a dusty Greyhound bus that was slow and making lots of noise. What a bad trip.

NEW KID

*T*here is a new kid on the block, and he's a top lawman who's slam-dunking women and refusing to recognize the chain of command. He walks in as if he's Paul Bunyan. He reaches out and grabs America because he can. He starts chopping down the Democratic Party. Why? Because it's music to the Republican Party, and he wants to see dancing in the streets. It's poetry all over again, and it's white male power. In fact, his enthusiasm seems to be potentially motivated to show disrespect for a black president, a black attorney general, and women in general.

Sorry, but it all appears to be about exerting power and turning back the hands of time to the "good old days," when a white male was never wrong in dealings with women and minorities. He has aligned himself with Donald Trump, the Sexy Guy, even though there are more women in America than men. There are a lot of women brainwashed, but it is my hope that women recognize how close they are to leveling the playing field. A vote for the Nice Lady, Hillary Clinton, will end most women's depression because it's good for self-esteem. So take a tip.

THE ADMINISTRATION MOVIE

*n*ever a dull moment, but sometimes it's hard to keep up with the characters in this movie. They seem to exit without warning. This movie is in the process of being rated. Excellent cast, starring the Sexy Guy and Anthony Scary Movie. I did a video on Anthony Scary Movie and the Sexy Guy. However, I have not released it because one of the stars of this show has been redirected (told to get lost). But let me tell you, I had some fun making that video. It had me laughing so badly until I almost cried at one point. I think it was probably a little bit funny. It was all about two guys having dinner while doing the Funky Broadway in an alley in New York City after the midnight hour (love birds). The theme song is "Cheating in the Next Room" by Johnny Taylor.

THE PINK PANTHER

*R*emember the cartoons that used to come on every Saturday morning? They were always fun and exciting. We didn't have cartoon channels during that time, and so Saturday was the big day because we got to see some of the greatest cartoons of all times. Some of those cartoons characters were so popular that the character starred in movie theaters. One of those cartoon characters was the Pink Panther, who was my favorite next to the Road Runner.

Okay, we have the scene, so let's compare. The committee chairman is equated to the Pink Panther. He's the whistleblower who blows on everyone, including himself. One thing you could always depend on, and that was, the Pink Panther stumbling into trouble. He never made sense—sort of like Daffy Duck.

THE BLACK PANTHER

*Y*ears ago, in the sixties in the Deep South, one of the most popular jobs during that time was driving a tractor. The competition was fierce—sort of like the house these days. My father use to tell a lot of jokes, but one stuck out. It was a strange story about a tractor driver whose name was never mentioned. I was a little boy who adored my father. This story he told me about this particular tractor driver was interesting because he got chased by a black panther.

It all started when the boss decided to clear more land that was back into the woods. He told the driver to stop work and get out to this particular field before dark. But there was some miscommunication that went on, because the man never left before dark. The man worked until the sun went down, and that's how this story begins. A black panther tore out from the trees, coming directly toward the driver. The driver jumped off the tractor and began to run. The man remembered hearing a group of older men talk about things that worked when chased by a black panther. He was instructed to start taking off clothes because the panther would stop and rip up every piece of clothing before continuing the chase. This story ends with the man getting away, but he was buck naked. The moral of the story is one must learn to follow before leading, taking matters into one's own hands.

WANDERING

*L*et's straighten it out. But always keep in mind, people, that God is love. If you have deviated from God's love or are not willing to align with the constitution, then you are no longer representing America. One must also understand that the Republican Party looks like a bunch of thugsand is in total disarray. Simply put, they don't represent America anymore. They have become so wishy-washy until it's an embarrassment. Plus, they don't believe in jobs bills being passed. It appears that the Republicans' main job for the last eight years was to obstruct a Democratic president in order to make him look bad, and to prevent any jobs bills from getting through. They are planning the same for Hillary Clinton. Wow. They don't care about the American people—every man or woman for himself or herself. Obama tried time and time again to get jobs bills passed. Deadbeat Congress was partying down with no. They were on vacation for eight years, and they all wore earplugs.

It's time now for the American people to get rid of those losers. They held the United States hostage for eight years. I don't want Donald Trump to be president. If you vote down ballot for those Republican clowns again, are you sure you love America? Also, I hope you don't need a job. The Republicans really mean to do nothing and block all jobs bills. We have had enough of these obnoxious people. Let's make sense and move on down the line. Let's all vote down ballot for the Democratic Party. That is the only way to move this country again. As for me, I will be training for a marathon soon. I heard that the marathon used to be 25 miles. Now it's 26.1 miles. The last mile was added on simply because the princess of England requested to see the finish line from the castle. Now, I have run several marathons, but I never fail to remember that princess in that last mile. She made a bad decision—I can attest to that!

BEST CANDIDATE

There was something about Senator John McCain, the gentlemen who ran for president against Senator Barack Obama, which we all understood, and we came to conclude that he was an outstanding gentleman. I would have voted for him if he hadn't been running against Barack. He would have been one of the greatest Republican presidents of all time, and his wife would have been a wonderful, classy first lady. He is still one of the best Republican candidates in America right now. We all love him and want to hear what he has to say. Everybody is squabbling over the president's health care plan, but remember that health plan started out in Massachusetts with the Republican Party. I think John would have implemented the same health plan as President Obama. He was a very smart man who understands and happens to be a very good debater—something Donald Trump never possessed.

Trump is the most terrible debater ever. He just came out and put down women, and he is still doing the same. There is a lot of fiddling and square dancing going on in Washington, DC these days—a hillbilly flip show. You have to be a shade tree man or woman in DC these days to sneak through real legislation. There are no directions, and everything is a sideshow, pure entertainment.

No Way

There has been a lot of talk in the news lately about racism in America, so let's go back down memory lane. Remember when summer vacation for blacks was only five weeks in the South? This was done so that blacks could pick cotton for the plantation owners. They sat in that hot school without air-conditioning for the rest of the summer. School was also out in October and November to pick cotton. These days, I hear a few whites speculating about whether blacks were better off during that time than now, or better off as slaves. Hey, please stop. I was there during the split summers and falls, and I hated it. I'm sure that slavery had to be much worse and could only be approved by the devil himself.

However, we were taught as kids to be nice and careful around white people to avoid trouble. I think some whites were naive to think that we liked their behavior—or even worse, were happy—making that trend of thought very psychotic. As a psychologist, I conclude that this is a great fabrication that has swept our nation and left behind a group of ignorant people. You would have to have a serious diagnosis like schizophrenia, or be suffering from psychosis, to even consider this type of thinking, which is altogether inappropriate. But I'm glad it's a topic of discussion nowadays.

STICKING TOGETHER

Hey, America, hang in there. I've got love for you, and your marching is on the mark. The Trump Administration welcomes us to Fool Land. Our country is being turned over to old folks who are suffering from amnesia and are one step away from a wheelchair. Their mission is impossible and flat-out crazy. Donald Trump doesn't have a clue about doing things in a respectful way—it's all done thuggish. He's an old man, already tired, and Alzheimer's has begun to set in because he doesn't remember what he has just said. It's too much of a task for anyone his age who has never governed before. Unpredictability, yes. However, call it what it is: forgetful. This is an unstable con man, and he is a mess. He doesn't need a chance to get better because he's already too far gone and crazy enough to destroy the world. Goodbye, Charlie.

HALLOWEEN

don't know what another therapist saw today, but as for me, I saw a group of Republicans standing behind and with a man who has an inferiority complex, and it's chronic. He's suffering from feelings of not measuring up to standards, and of desperately needing to succeed and be better than others, especially the previous president.

It's plainly a lack of self-worth that produces doubt and uncertainty about this guy. It is mostly a subconscious thing, but it is a force that drives afflicted individuals like him to overcompensate to the point of insanity, while focused on getting results in a desire to always seek after spectacular achievements. But one usually ends up depressed or displaying asocial behavior. So in order to avoid depression, he lies, manipulates, cheats, and does just about anything to keep the attention on himself. His life is one impulsive Chattanooga Choo Choo train. He pressures others to fulfill his needs, and it's at all costs. Oftentimes it's against humanity—there aren't any norms. Nothing is done by this individual on the behalf of others, because he is selfish and can never be trusted.

GROUND HOG DAY

This is an American fantasy comedy movie. It's about a weatherman who was sent to the same location four years in a row to cover the same event: Groundhog Day. It took place in the same small town. Well, apparently this weatherman didn't see this event as credible enough for a reporter of his status. It was obvious that he hated the assignment. But here is where it gets weird. Upon awaking the next day, he discovers that it's Groundhog Day all over again. The same day keeps repeating itself time and time again. First he uses this to his advantage, and then he succumbs to the realization that he is doomed to spend the rest of eternity in the same place, seeing the same people every day.

As I recall, it was so different from any other movie we had ever seen. The actor relived the same day over and over again. Every morning he would wake up and relive the same day as before. Here is the kicker: he lived that day for so long until it made no difference what happened that particular day. He knew he would relive that same day the very next day. Doesn't that ring a bell? No matter what happens, the same day is being relived over and over again with the Trump Administration. America is dancing to an old, crazy beat. I know it's steady stepping backward. I think it's stepping in the wrong direction. Our song today is "Hit the Road, Jack" by Ray Charles.

HOLD YOUR HORSES

*D*onald Trump is not concerned with the health of the American people. Be careful when playing with nutty people. They don't think things through. It's like dealing with stupid and desperate people who come up with bad ideas on a regular basis. It's a white male thing that's designed to hurt woman and people of color. They take pleasure in hurting the vulnerable as always, going back in time. It's a power shift, women, and you lose. So be careful guarding Obama's health care. To be safe, get a bulldog grip.

JIGSAW PUZZLE

*T*he Trump Administration is constantly dropping clues here and there about what Donald Trump is saying, or meant to say, through telepathy communications, better known as mind reading. Nostradamus would be confused. These prognosticators are skilled in wishy-washy with fantasy views. Donald Trump's strike in Syria seemed iffy; it was like a person going rabbit hunting in the desert. Others would say that it was like a person throwing a brick at a bird flying overhead. I thought in a situation like that, it would be considered an act of war. Now, in war the ideal is to destroy the enemy. You don't call ahead and make reservations, and give the time and location of the strike. Because if you do, then it's a visit.

Well, we understand this act of treason. America, hold on and keep praying, because this is our country. This guy has rolled back many things that his predecessor had carefully thought out and put into place, all for the good of the country. Donald Trump doesn't even know what he is signing. This moron has created a mess in our country, and in time it will show what a loser he really is. When he says "our country," what country is that? The over-the-hill gang in 1959, or a close tie with a foreign country? No one knows how to put his jigsaw mind together;

Hidden Knowledge 83

it's like Humpty Dumpty after the fall. To true Americans: let's push for truth and righteousness for our country. Our good will over power this jigsaw man, because he's slow at remembering just about anything discussed.

Dr. Oscar McKinley

LAUGH OUT LOUD

*I*t was poetry in motion today, and the suspense was over whelming and appalling. Donald Trump made his move. In all actuality, it was a walk back down crazy lane. Negativity filled the air—sort of like the sinking of the *Titanic*, which was not a good place to be. Donald Trump was wheeling and dealing in Washington, DC, threatening every weak Republican in his path. He proved today that he is not a deal maker, just another simple loser lacking knowledge. I'm positive about that, because he ended up going down the drain. Call a plumber!

This guy is miserable and desperate. He never stands up like a man. He's always blaming someone else for his shortcomings, which is creating some serious psychological behavior among staff members. What's up with all of this espionage? I'm wonder how many more are in the White House. Maybe ten? Why can't we put an end to it before it's too late? Who's preventing us from stopping it? We know that Donald Trump likes to control people. Does anyone really believe he didn't know exactly what was going on? Democrats are smart enough to get to the bottom of this nightmare, but whose side are the Republicans on? It doesn't appear like it's America's. This should be dealt with first.

I try to learn something new every day. Today, I learned today that

Nancy Pelosi is one of the smartest people in Washington. She gave an answer that slammed the door in the Republicans' faces. When she was asked who the leaders of the Democratic Party was, she stated, "President Obama and Secretary Clinton are still the leaders of the Democratic Party." Keep letting it roll.

MISTAKEN IDENTITY

*E*very time there seems to be a genuinely clear diagnosis after noting the behavior, something else emerges with similarities that are still creepy, and it's another spooky character, but altogether it's a different diagnosis. I have counted five. It's far out on a limb, but who cares? America must have it coming. Some people voted for Donald Trump, and now they are standing by watching as he tries to turn America into a Banana Republic. He's only focused on destroying his predecessor's accomplishments. So keep an eye on this guy rolling back everything. It's absolutely preposterous to see a president so unprepared. This snatch-and-grab guy has turned the White House into a psychedelic shack. The kids only visit when he's gone. He's imitating the reincarnation of bad, bad Leroy Brown, the meanest and baddest cat in the whole damn town. He's badder than old King Kong and meaner than a junkyard dog.

That's who he thinks he is, but that's a mistaken identity. Here is who he really is: Tweety Bird from Looney Tunes. So let's call him an atrocious cool cat, trying to steal America's gold. Hey, we are forgetting one thing? It doesn't snow in the summer here, and another president ultimately follows this guy. Will that person demand the same kind of treatment, or more? Wow, what does America do then? Oh, I know: cry yourself to sleep at night. It's the Republicans who created this monster, but the shoe will be on the other foot someday.

What is it about California? Kamala Harris and Maxine Waters are creating a tornado in Washington, DC. These ladies are heroes and deserve our respect. They are tough enough, are Wonder Women. Wait a minute— let's count Elizabeth Warren too. Make it triplets!

THE REAL JESUS

*M*egan Kelly had an embarrassing moment on national television when she alleged, "Kids, Santa Clause is white." That was a serious blunder. I laugh because I know the person who was referred to as Santa Clause was black. However, the truth has been hidden because of the slave owners, and later the hate groups, intimidating people with violence and forcefully brainwashing people in America. They're making it look like the white man did everything. No, I'm not that stupid, boss. Now, here is the greatest blunder of all time: that Jesus Christ was a white man. That's impossible because no whites lived in the Holy Land during that time.

Those of us who know better see a fractured environment in America filled with stupidity, which is the main problem. Leonardo da Vinci painted a portrait of a white man off the streets named Cesare and called him Jesus Christ. The white male in America used that portrait to manipulate all Americans to believe that this was Jesus Christ. There is no need to be ignorant anymore. This should not be kept secret: Jesus was a man of color (black). It's very strange to still see black people posting pictures of this white man and calling him Jesus. Jesus had to be a man of color, and the Bible explains that. If you want the truth, seek it. Now, to white Christians,

God is not in this type of mess. A fake, white-man portrait of his son? To be honest, I think this slavery thing was sick, and any fools who want to reinforce this type of mess need the real Jesus and some serious therapy, because they are crazy as hell. Our song today is "People Get Ready" by Curtis Mayfield.

Dr. Oscar McKinley

How Jews Became White

*m*aurice Fishberg wrote an article called "Physical Anthropology of the Jews—Pigmentation."

It all came about with the scattering of Jews. The blond traits originated through interactional marriages, bringing about an infusion of Jewish blood into the veins of the modern-day Jewish people, because they look white. Okay, the original Jew was black, but some have changed through the years. Let the truth be told. White people know this, and they also know how Jews really became white in the country of Russia. It's very easy to trace. Even today, Jews are not considered white, but they have white skin. That's why the Nazis and hate groups in Charlottesville were specifying in their chanting that Jews would not take their place: because they resembled whites. Let me add that it also includes one-third black Americans, who really are the original Jews. This thing should not be kept secret anymore, but be discussed in detail how Jews became white and who black American people really are.

You can trace this for yourself. There should be no more pretending, because all hate groups are aware and are being taught the truth. This is what it's all about: hidden identity. Well, let's let God handle his business. He's the creator, not us. God did not create gods here on earth, because he's

God alone. God and his son, Jesus, are not angry with Jews, because they are the chosen race. Jesus doesn't operate through hate; he gets his point across through peace and love.

Now, people seeking control is a different story or thing altogether. It has nothing to do with representing God. It's a deceitful and evil act that's designed to manipulate confused people and teach hate. It's insinuating that God can't make it on his own without you. The song of today is "Another Blessing" by Melvin and Lee Williams.

SUPER FLY

*N*ow, wait. In one of my writings, I explained that Donald Trump was flexible enough to be a black street man. Let's give him credit: he might be the gorgeous Super Fly. It appears that he has the credentials. It was always splendid and grand while watching him search for more money and women. What an inflated ego. His theme song is "Super Fly" by Curtis Mayfield. Throwing women under the bus is protocol; it's traditionalism. In his world, the sun doesn't rise without his permission, because it's an extreme fantasy land like a cartoon character. I'm sure he doesn't know God, and that's why he's still ignorant.

The question is, will he ever understand why America is great and respected? It's really comical watching him bully and manipulate people day after day. I think all inner-city black men understand this guy. He's following the guidelines of the ghetto code of ethics: gotta be a macho man. Also, please keep in mind that the repeal of Obamacare was suggested years ago out of meanness, rebelling against a black president.

FAKE COLORS

et's learn a little bit today about the term "white people." It all started in Europe, somewhere in the late seventeenth century. But it was already a movement that had begun in the 1500s. Remember the painting of Jesus? Europeans began to develop an alignment of racism, which was done to connect biological traits rather than cultural ones. They wanted a name for all European populations to merge into a single race, called white. In America, slave owners took this white thing and ran with it—simply because the Bible stated that white was pure and blessed. It became a weapon used on slaves. Okay, let's look at this. When the Bible was written, there wasn't a white person around to contribute anything to its writing. All the people were black. So when they mention white in the Bible as pure and in a good way, it wasn't about people, but about cleanliness. It's easy to see dirt on white, and *white* wasn't used for race until the 1700s.

Racism went into everything afterward, even religion. Restricting blacks with church rules and regulations pointed to white superiority (manmade, not God). I think the scary part is that most whites do not want the truth. They entertain any kind of fake news that favors them. No race is superior; otherwise, God would not have created us as equal. Africa was the richest continent on earth a thousand years ago. European scientists wrote in the 1700s and 1800s that there was major a difference between black and white people, and they gave fake reasons why the whites had superiority over blacks. Maybe that's why a law was passed in America to prevent blacks from reading and writing: to hide the truth. Our song today is "Touch a Hand, Make a Friend" by the Staple Singers.

FORREST GUMP

It's unbelievable that there's a person like Forrest Gump in the White House, which is nothing more than a hideout these days. It's impossible for the Sexy Guy, Donald Trump, to straighten up and fly right, because of his superior genes malfunctioning like a hillbilly's dance. No one understands what he's doing except for maybe a time traveler. It's weird but sophisticated and nice, like smart slave owners who believe in the superiority of the white race and think they're highly intelligent over blacks. The Bible said to resist the devil, and he will flee from you. Donald Trump and his white skin worshipers are misguiding America and have abandon God. Our song today is "If You're Ready (Come Go with Me)" by the Staple Singers. No time to pussyfoot around, because God's watching.

WAKE UP, EVERYBODY

*A*ll right, I think it's a beautiful thing to recognize the inside beauty of another person; it's incredible. Let's take it a step further and go into the spiritual world. Remember that God's Spirit looks on the heart. When you connect with the beauty inside another person, it makes you and that person become one. But the strange thing about this connection is that the doors entering this connection must always be open to all people. Stay away from judging if you can. This connection is crucial to one's growth because without it, a person will never learn to respect and appreciate oneself and will never understand the power of diversity. Stop and think.

That brings me to my point. There is something negative going on at 1600 Pennsylvania Avenue, known as the museum of the cocoon that's housing the swamp creature. It's like Pee Wee's "Monster in the Playhouse." The thrill is gone from there, and it's a gloomy situation. Let's pray for them. Also, please be aware that some of them are not trained; it's almost like dealing with a rattle snake. Now, wisdom is the principle thing to get, but understanding takes priority. To be safe, let's just follow the Yellow Brick Road. This playhouse is orbiting the planet, and there is no connection with the people on earth; they're lost in space. When people try to connect with these individuals in Pee Wee's Playhouse, keep in mind that the people inside are entrenched in hatred, are oblivious to common sense, and take pride in being a ghetto gangster. Okay, now, let's pass the word. Our song is "Wake Up, Everybody" by Teddy Pendergrass, Harold Melvin, and the Blue N.

I Dreamed of a Genie

dream is an act taking place within our minds while we are asleep, and we have absolutely no control over what goes on. However, we as humans are always influenced by our dreams. They are usually about something we fear, heard about, or saw. But sometimes we can use our imaginations within our dreams, and that's strange. Now, dreams can be very confusing and even frightening. Ultimately, dreams must be genuinely resolved in a disproportionate way. One of the greatest stories ever told about mysterious dreams happened to Pharaoh in Egypt. It was written in the Old Testament. It all started when a young boy named Joseph was sold into slavery by his brothers at the age of seventeen. But Joseph had the gift of interpreting dreams. As the story goes, Joseph interpreted Pharaoh's dream. By doing so, he was promoted from slavery to second in command of Egypt.

It is said that the subconscious mind in most cases is much wiser that the conscience. I think this points to what the Bible means about not letting the sun go down on your anger. Because anger does negative things to the subconscious mind, it tortures one in one's sleep. We should have a peaceful sleep without negative interference. Now, I think humans process information based on how well we allowed our dreams to progress. There are several psychologists who formulated their own opinions about this matter. But I think Jesus was the greatest psychologist of all times. Jesus sort of let us figure out most things on our own, but he drops clues along the way, like when the rich man came to Jesus and asked what he must do to be saved. Jesus gave a strange answer that totally went over the man's head. Jesus told him to go give everything he owned away and then come back. I think he wanted the man to change his focus. Seeking wealth can dominate one's mind to focus only on getting more. They don't see the poor as humans, and neither do they care what happens to them or try to understand their needs. Jesus wanted him to struggle and see the world from a different perspective. Only then could the rich man understand what Christianity was all about.

There are a lot of people who think success is better than a real relationship with God. They want to be notice and seek praises. This puts constant pressure on the people surrounding them. But the praises should be for God. The Scripture says that God love praises. I think when man seeks and develops a need for praises, he is no longer sound enough to understand his surroundings, and he adopts the empty wagon syndrome. A true leader always puts the spotlight on others.

Okay, let's have some fun. Let's pretend that Donald Trump happens to find a bottle in the Oval Office that has a genie inside. The genie pops out and recognizes the problems going on, and it immediately suggests everyone in the room can be granted one wish. There are three people in the room: Donald Trump, Jeff Sessions, and Paul Ryan. Jeff wishes for a new tractor with a bubble gum machine on board, and it appears. Paul wishes to have a life of "Can't We All Just Get Along." The genie sends him to hell. Then the final wish comes from Donald Trump. He wishes things were normal at the White House. Without hesitation, President Obama appears. Our song for today is "I'll Take You There" by the Staple Singers.

CHRISTIAN VALUES

hristians are people who embrace the teachings of Jesus. One of the first things we learn as Christians is to not take revenge, because God said that vengeance was his. Donald Trump mistakenly overlooked that, because he takes pride in revenge. The second thing we learn is to try the Spirit by the word. Trump falls short again because he doesn't deny himself, and it appears that he sees himself as God. The list goes on, but you might find this interesting. Jesus said, "You will know my followers by the way they treat the least among you." We know Donald Trump wants to take away people's health care and let them die. It's not something that Jesus would ever consider. Jesus cared about people suffering, and especially the poor.

Donald Trump is an unstable white man playing the role of the white savior. His goal is to erase every deed of his predecessor, who happened to be black. It's shameful and disgraceful that America has this debilitating man supposedly sent by God, which is surely fake news. Yes, it's only an act of white supremacy. Plus, it's obvious he's a racist and is actively encouraging a race war, which is demonic and pure evil. It's the same approach as Hitler. The question is, did God send Hitler? The answer is no. This guy lies just as Hitler did, and he also wants to take control of other countries, starting with Venezuela and other South American countries. Do Christians believe in stealing and taking away other countries' wealth?

I have been saved for over thirty-five years and went to Bible college with mostly whites. We had to go to church almost every day. I have never seen white Christians act like this. They are mysteriously strange these days. I don't recognize a lot of them anymore because they are not following Jesus. I have one question for them. What are *your* Christian values? Our song today is "Precious Lord, Take My Hand" by Mahalia Jackson.

THE GREAT CIVIL RIGHTS LEADER

*K*eep in mind that we had an America president, governors, senators, and representatives who were black. Now, Dr. Martin Luther King was neither, yet he was the true leader. I wouldn't worry about who's the leader of the Democratic Party. That person is probably sitting back and smiling. I believe the right people will step up when it's time. But in the meantime, listen to "Make Yours a Happy Home" by Gladys Knight and the Pips. Remember, we were dealt a hand from the bottom of the deck, and it's called cheating. At the same time, these people have put a mortgage on the United States of America. They are pirates and are busy stealing.

Let's straighten out the cards this time. There is nothing to worry about within the Democratic Party. But we need to push harder and keep an eye on the deck. To this president, every day is an adventure in the Twilight Zone, and it's not science fiction but psychological horror. However, America will be solid again, and Jove will prevail, so let's stay vigilant and continue to hold hands.

RIP VAN WINKLE

I like telling stories. I find the best storytellers always use an innovative tone to introduce original and creative thinking, which is usually presented through voice. Well, here we go again, but a little time off was really needed. I think most of us have read, heard, or seen a movie about Rip Van Winkle. Just to update you on Old Rip, he's the guy who fell asleep in the mountains and slept through the Revolutionary War. When he awakens, Rip discovers drastic changes have taken place, and he notices strange things took place with his weapon as well as his looks. His beard comes down to his waist, and he notices that he feels tired. He returns to his village and finds that he cannot recognizes anyone. But there is something strange going on in the village. People keep coming up to him and asking who he voted for in the presidential election. Old Rip has no idea what a vote is, and so he proclaims himself a faithful subject of King George, unaware of the great struggle that took place called the American Revolution. It got him in a bit of trouble. Poor Rip, lost in time.

Can you imagine the horrendous damage Rip would cause if he became president after waking up, lost in time? The world will always be flat. We have a similar scenario in America these days, because of Donald Trump as the president, sounding like an intelligent empty wagon that's stuck in a broken time machine. It's catastrophically amiss and must be abandoned, simply because it's the wrong country. It is the epitome of a rock-bottom functioning that's like the Flintstones. Hey, Democrats, hold on tight and keep flying above the storm, like an eagle cruising in flight. Move through time wide awake, alert, and focused, always pushing hard. Our song today is "Better Be Good to Me" by Tina Turner.

STOP AND THINK

When something bad has happened to you, and the thoughts keep reoccurring, stop and think. Sometimes people going through this phase replay events over and over in their minds, using different scenarios. But if the event that's triggering the stress is devastating enough, they can't break free of the high stress on their own. They will need professional help. It becomes PTSD, and it's a very serious diagnosis because it keeps reoccurring on a regular basics, creating tremendous stress. It can be an event, but it can also be a person like the Sexy Guy, Donald Trump. Republicans need to understand that the Sexy Guy frightens people and stresses a whole nation. We are turning into a nation filled with a host of PTSD candidates. It's all because of his unstable behavior.

America isn't recognizable enough for our kids to grasp anymore. These are dedicated American families who have not done anything wrong and who love this country, but the Sexy Guy doesn't care about the American people. This guy acts like a kid in the playground, and kids recognize that he's unfit. On the one hand, Senator Get Well had it right when he stated that the Asian leader was just a fat kid who was making noise and didn't understand what he was saying or doing. On the other hand, the Sexy Guy is a bigger kid and is not as mature as the Asian leader—ice cream for two. Keep in mind that it's normal for this Asian group of people to be under this type of stress; they know how to deal with something of this magnitude. A nutty leader is common for them, and they have learned to accept ignorance. They are a country cut off from the world and lacking understanding, so what this administration is saying to them is not resonating. It's like Granny from *The Beverly Hillbillies,* threatening Duke the dog. Americans don't need this stress, so let's put an end to it. The Sexy Guy is still trying to fulfill his fantasy that he's magnificent, which is considered crazy.

A tip to this administration: please stop selling wolf tickets; that Asian country is too stupid to understand clowning around. The previous president ignored most of their behavior because their leader is a kid who's throwing a temper tantrum. Adults should understand how kids are almost always in the rebellion stage. I hope this administration isn't stupid enough to put nuclear weapons on the table—that's pure insanity. It sounds like crazy people talking, with everything on the table. Good God almighty, how long will this nut balling go on? The black man said, "Can't we all just get along?"

The Mountaintop View

*L*et's make more statues and monuments. I have two great Americans in mind who stood for the Union, under the United States flag, and who deserve statue after statue. They brought about true change for the betterment of humankind. They're two of the greatest men I have ever laid my eyes upon. They both held the office of president of the United States of America. Let's go with President Barack Obama and President Lyndon B. Johnson. They are two of the best. How lucky are some of us to have seen them both? Let's lift them up, because they are magnificent men. Thank God. A dedicated song is "Fire and Rain" by James Taylor.

AMERICAN NAZI OR CONFEDERATE

*G*od bless Texas. We love you all. Hold on. We were taught as marines that if you ever get separated from your unit, to stay put. Somebody is coming to get you, because we work together. I can remember sitting in front of the television as a kid, watching the richest man in the world out of Texas being interviewed by a news reporter. The reporter stated, "Man, you have it made. You're the richest man in the world." The rich man replied, "No, sir, I don't. I still have to work with people." I equate that answer to King David of the Scriptures. David said, "I can't get away from God, no matter where I go." Solomon requested to be able to go in and out before the people—very wise. That's the key to being a public servant.

I recently saw an interview on national television coming out of Texas about this black man saving the life of a white man who had a Confederate flag. I'm a little dismayed at why some people are still struggling over flags that don't have a country. We as Americans pledge our allegiance to the flag of the United States of America, and to the republic for which it stands, one nation under God, indivisible, with liberty and justice for all. If I'm not mistaken, every country only has one flag. Now, I heard people chanting from the hate groups that they wanted their country back. Okay, but blacks read and write these days, and so that may be impossible to achieve. All right, let's say that the Confederates got their thirteen Southern states back. How do you deal with the many races? As for the swastika flag, it's illegal to fly in Germany, and there is no place for that mess here in America.

I'm a psychologist, and my goal is to understand all human behavior. I hold a double doctorate in special education and psychology with a degree in religion. I graduated with a 3.98 GPA. I had two chairs while writing my dissertation, and it was tough; I worked night and day on that dissertation. I suffered between those two chairs because they both requested things from me that were entirely different from the other. But I had to work with those two men until we were all on the same page. It required subordinate behavior until I knew exactly how to proceed, and then we were a team. Now, when Senator Duckworth's helicopter went down, we would have been first to get her out. What a brave woman, to fly into the danger zone. I love her because she was really protecting this country. She's a wonderful American. We pledged our allegiance to one flag and to one nation under God. Our song for today is the national anthem, "The Star-Spangled Banner."

MEMORIES

*A*nthony *Bourdain: Parts Unknown* showed a series that included President Obama tonight in Hanoi, Vietnam. The president was visiting there last year, and the scene was so cool. When the president pulled up, a James Brown song was playing, "Paying the Cost to Be the Boss." I remember the first time I saw that series, and the feeling was euphoric. The nation was safe, and all was secure. America, as well as the rest of the world, enjoyed a golden age under President Obama. Now, the feeling is always unrest—fake news and lie after lie. This president is flat-footed, nuking around. It's maniac time, 100 percent *Silence of the Lambs*.

No

*L*et's help Donald Trump with his approval ratings. It means more to him than America. We don't want to say one of his favorite things, "witch hunt." He likes witches for some strange reason. Please change your vocabulary, guy. Now, here is the truthful approval rating for the Sexy Guy. It's between 13 and 17 percent on the real side, and that's counting the boondocks. We are not giving him credit for his lack of skills. No more petting his ego. He's doing a terrible job and should leave, because he isn't capable of getting better. All middle-class and poor people are doomed—he really hates them. Most of the Republican senators are up for sale, and the owner is Donald Trump.

INSTITUTIONALIZED VIOLENCE IN AMERICA

t has caught up, and is now a reality for all Americans, that we as a nation are endeavoring for views that employ violence. Depending on one's standpoint, most sociologist and psychologists would say that we are legitimizing violent behavior because it's Donald Trump view. His administration understands institutionalized violence because they are partakers. But they are not able to completely acknowledge the facts that they are the racist engine behind the violence in America. They want to make-believe they are undercover guys. There is no difference between these men and those poor, sick, hateful people on the streets in Virginia today. Because their intentions are the same: attack women and people of color. They are practicing terrorism through intimidation. Their rule of thumb is putting fear into people, which is hate groups' favorite tactic. So look out, Christians—you are losing what God supposedly gave you. It takes more than saying, "The devil made me do it." There are added psychological things going on with Donald Trump, like Asperger's factor ASD, which includes difficulty socializing and making friends. One may also have a speaking problem. Our song today is "A Change Is Gonna Come" by Sam Cooke.

SOPHISTICATED WOLF

*M*ost of us have read the scriptures about the controversial undercover costume of a wolf coming in sheep's clothing as a deception to steal the flock. It's sort of like April Fool's Day. Well, get a load of this: let's try a new scenario using the sheep's clothing. Let's say Donald Trump's sheep clothing is white skin, which makes him more difficult to be spotted, because in America most people are looking for the wolf to look different from the color white, which usually tricks people into letting him into their homes. The Bible states that white is pure. I wonder if that means all white skin is good?

There is a lot of howling going on these days at the White House. We know for sure it's filled with wolves. They are howling night and day, dogging us around. They are walking the dog (a wolf) twenty-four hours per day. This wolf is dangerous, and he's proposing to discourage all Americans and eventually abolish our way of life. It's a family business. The world will now know all of America's secrets, because it's the mission of the Trump Administration to destroy our government. We must face this evil force now. Let's change the job description from what we had. It read, "Job opening at the White House for president of the United States of America. No experience needed. We welcome psychotic behavior and would love for you to tell us lies on a daily basis. We love wonderful fake news. Bonus points: please have a spy crew available to deliver our secrets to foreign governments."

GOTTA HOLD ON TO
THIS FEELING

*I*t's becoming apparent that America as a whole is actually in a large therapy session. We are no longer pretending to hide how we feel about race. I feel that can be an innovative, positive thing—as long as it's not elevated to hate. Hate does horrendous damage to one's soul, and it cuts off the learning process of human growth. Hate allows people to see what's important for them and no other races, directly contradicting the constitution and what it stands for. But slowly people are coming to the realization that the Republican Party does not share their values and is no longer aligned with hard-working Americans. However, it does specifically reveal similarities that are parallel to the wealthy. It's ominously bothering the country as a whole.

We can no longer be sympathetic to unpopular views. People during the sixties had it right, and we need to revisit their philosophy that calm the nation through peace and love. Their way of life was impervious to hate, and they honored love, peace, and joy, which brought happiness throughout our nation. Our song today is "Way Back Home" by Jr. Walker and the All Stars.

Now, can I do a little comedy? It's flooding and pouring rain all over the United States of America, and we don't have but one raincoat. Let's put it on justice, not the jokers. We still own America the Beautiful. But it's a hound dog thing these days. However, it's still left up to we the people. Our song today is "Gotta Hold on to This Feeling" by Walker and the All Stars.

WHATCHA SAY?

*D*onald Trump was in Saudi Arabia preaching love and togetherness like a Muslim baptism preacher. He was on the right subject with the love thing. I got that one. However, it had to be an overnight revelation with a certain inspiration that inspired him on the flight there. Because he didn't preach love, peace, and togetherness before he left. To be accurate, it was actually the direct opposite. He's a two-faced rascal. As for Americans, our song is "Move on Up" by Curtis Mayfield.

Macho Man of 2017

*N*one other than Senator John McCain holds the title of macho man of the year. Now, that's corn bread, greens, and banana pudding. Man, your style mesmerizes us. Goodness gracious, man, you're super bad. It's like looking at a gladiator in live action, as smooth as the morning sunlight. The two lady senators aren't far behind. Let's say it loud: they're women and proud. It's time for a woman to be president, and I can't hardly wait. It's women's power now, guys, so move over. Today's song is "Float On" by the Floaters. Oh, as far as I'm concerned, John McCain is my president. I'll fly with you any day you choose, John.

POKÉMON

ey, guys, remember that cotton field? God taught us how to respect people and survive wickedness day after day. It was steadfastness, and we knew how to do it—a piece of cake. But to be honest, no one in American knows how to do it like a woman. They go into the delivery room while men wait outside. Women are strong and getting stronger by the day. I wonder if we can lean on you. I believe in you and recognize your powers. Now evolve, ladies, like a Pokémon. And remember Pokémon took over television like a storm. I know because I used to watch. I'm going to go out on a limb and say soon women will rule the world, probably for the next one hundred years. (Yes, you can!) Our song is Tyrone Davis's "Be Honest with Me."

TWEETER DEMAGOGUE

Watching a wrestling match is like watching sports without rules. It's like being one-on-one with Donald Trump. They bite, hit, kick, use chairs, fist, and use practically anything they get their hands on. But it's all fake. Kids don't know it's fake, and neither do immature adults. They think it's real. Now, for adults to think that way, it's probably because of cell damage, or being unable to disguise motives. Donald Trump can put a move on you out of this world, sort of like Houdini escaping a straitjacket. He loves to wrestle; it's grabbing time for him, just like a rooster in the barnyard. Race is his calling card to distribute hate.

He's recruiting white intelligent people who are unable to understand the difference between right and wrong. He will teach you to hate at a level never seen before. He's guaranteed to be a hellcat showing the racist card. At the bottom of humanity, where there aren't any rules, plenty of stupid politicians belong to him. He's the director, star, and producer of this unlimited chaos. I guess you can say that we are all enrolled in Trump University and are being held hostage by this tyrant. Dance with me; the music is Tina Turner's "Simply the Best."

MISSISSIPPI FOOTBALL

'm coming to Mississippi at the end of the month to see a football game. I will attend with my brother Richard. We are going to see Mississippi Valley State versus Jackson State, and hopefully we'll enjoy the bands at halftime. I would love to get a chance to see some of my friends at the game. Our song today is "The Thrill Is Gone" by BB King and Bobby Blue Bland.

THE BRIDGE OVER
TROUBLE WATER

I pray to God to have mercy on America and deliver us from this horrific evil that's causing horror to our nation. I pray for all the families who are suffering from the loss of their loved ones, and for others who have lost all their possessions. We are in unmeasured territory, surrounded by strange events that are too horrible to imagine. Peace, love, and togetherness are what God wants. The Bible states that the fear of God is the beginning of knowledge, but there is a contrast, and it's that we shall not fear man.

We made a serious mistake, and so let's rectify it before it's too late. Donald Trump is distant and unapproachable, and on top of that, he wants to destroy America. We can't pretend that it doesn't matter. Remember in the Scriptures the two women who brought the baby before Solomon, both claiming to be the baby's mother? Solomon said cut the baby in half and give each mother half. One of the women said okay, let's do that. Immediately Solomon knew who the baby's mother was. It was the one who said, "No, don't cut the baby. Give the baby to her."

Well, we can use that same scenario here in America, because we have some whites who feel if they can't have America the way it was before President Obama, then they would rather see America destroyed. Now, that's not love for your country. Donald Trump is trying to change every single thing or sabotage all recorded accomplishments of the previous president He's Dr. Evil minus good luck. Be careful and move swiftly before the jackrabbit strikes again. I truly believe people are better off dealing with their fears than reacting to the fears.

I'll tell you a story about one of my fears. Most of us know the name and location of the most famous bridge in the world. Let me give you a hint: it's in California. All other bridges that were built before this bridge were a dark color, but this bridge had a loud, reddish orange color. Yes, it's the Golden Gate Bridge. Well, I had a unique experience with that bridge. I remember the first time I crossed it. All I could think about was the movie *Superman*, because in the movie, one of the huge cables broke on the bridge. This bus filled with kids was hanging over the side of the bridge, and Superman was nowhere to be found. It's the Superman movie that came out in 1977, and it was about a year later that I crossed the bridge. I didn't realize it at the time, but that movie had transcended my fears of a cable breaking, and so when I started to cross, all I felt were negative vibes, which shook me a little. I always try to control my fears, but that bridge got my attention. When I reached the other side, I parked and stared at that bridge for maybe an hour, trying to work through those feelings. Superman did a job on me. I decided to drive back across and come again. I ended up making several trips back and forth. After a while, I accomplished my mission. Let's work through these fears. All we have to do is focus and understand we can do it. No matter what it takes, we will not let those people destroy us or America. Our song is "City of New Orleans."

GILLIGAN'S ISLAND

illigan's Island was a television show that ran for quite a while in the sixties and seventies. It's about a group of people who rented a tourist boat for one day and ended up in a hurricane. They got lost at sea and came upon this small island that's not marked on any maps. No one would ever suspect to look for them there, simply because the island wasn't known to exist. They ended up having to make do with only the things that were on the island, and they had no outside contact. I really think Donald Trump confused Puerto Rico with Gilligan's Island. Most of us know where Puerto Rico is located and the type of transportation used to get there. "Where is the out there, ocean big water"—that's slang talk to the max, or I skipped English class. True Americans could only think of helping those people, not the NFL and arguments about the flag or who's disrespected it. I'm sure the people of Puerto Rico feel disrespected.

It took a while to resonate with Old Sexy. He was busy with dog whistles, which wasn't appropriate because of the serious nature of this matter. Thank God that the military is there now. But let's get back to the NFL and Donald. It appears that he wants the owners to stop paying black men millions. As the Sexy Guy put it, "I'm not happy with scared white men giving away big, beautiful money." Well, print the twenty-dollar bill of Harriet Tubman and let the NFL pass. It's not on the agenda. Hello, Rachael, nice hearing from you. Do you like *Family Feud*?

An update on Donald Trump's impulsiveness and absolutes. Rachael's impulsiveness for this guy is displayed through tone, urgency, and attitude. It's all illogical behavior and is totally without contemplating consequences. He always appears to be in a hurry during this stage, which makes him dangerously aggressive. That leads me to know that it was something recently said that triggered him. That NFL thing wasn't planned for that particular day. It's not Donald Trump's approach, and I know his behavior well. However, I do agree with you about his plan to attack the NFL, but at a different time; the wrong demeanor was present. He called NFL players sons of bitches. I have been studying this guy for a while. He and I dance a lot. You cut in with the wrong beat. Rachael, I think it's important for us to stay focus on Harriet Tubman's twenty-dollar bill. Next week is promising, Rachael. Have a good one. Our song is Tina Turner's "I Don't Wanna Fight Anymore."

ALABAMA

When we were kids growing up in Mississippi, every week night at 8:00 p.m., we would listen to the radio. This DJ called John R would always say, "This is John R way down south in Dixie." I liked to hear him say it. He made his voice sound black. He played all-black music, and he rocked. Can you dig it? As a kid in Mississippi, he was called the good white man. He kept hope alive in many blacks toward whites. Thanks to him, a seed was planted.

I want to talk today about Southern whites, so let's put on our thinking caps and jump back into time. Now, let's see if we can do a little brainstorming on the real side, but the first one must be free of animosity. You can't think clear when entangled with hate, deceit, or anger. I'm a psychologist, and my goal is to understand all human behavior. Remember that Jesus told the crowd if there were anyone among them without sin, let him cast the first stone.

All right, now let's get down to business and tell it like it is. The Southern white male has been nervous for a long time, and a high percentage doesn't trust God to keep them safe. He has made a lot of enemies, but not the white female. So in order to keep her thinking as he does, he projects his fears onto her. That confuses and frightens her, and so she aligns herself with him, not aware he's controlling her by keeping her scared. This guy running for the senate pulls a pistol on stage. He wants to make her think she's in danger, which is a lying deception. Donald Trump's whole conversation is about keeping America safe while always using the scared tactic. He shouldn't feel the need to say it over and over again. I think she fell for that lie because she resembles him. But the facts are she's innocent and didn't have anything to do with the cruelty of slavery and the shameful laws in America—it's a white male thing.

It's true that the white female is the greatest threat to a white male, and he knows it. But she doesn't, which creates his avenue of deception and attack civil rights. You see, she struggled to just vote, and she got her civil rights on the backs of mostly poor, uneducated, black Southerners. Now, why she aligns herself with the same white male is a mystery to me. But being realistic, she might notice that her way of life is tied in with American blacks—civil rights. The question remains, will she recognize her strengths, or will she continue to put her rights at risk with people like the senate guy and Donald Trump, the Creepy Crawlers? Well, here we go. Our song today is Marvin Gaye's "Let's Get It On."

MIRROR REFLECTION

I have written many things about my dad. His complexion made him look like a white man. There were advantages in Mississippi for those features, so I guess I grew up with special privileges and was sheltered somewhat from racism because of him. I recognized it, but I hated it because it gave me an advantage. I believe this administration wants blacks to step off the sidewalk whenever they pass. Nothing is actually fair; they seek the upper hand, and their world is completely filled with only white people. That should be a miserable feeling, because it's going against God as well as the constitution. They bully people and have demolished our constitution, and it has led to an enmeshment of renegades. There is no longer a balance in the senate because Trump has reduced our powerful Republican senators to kids on the playground calling names.

Our first song today is Bonnie Tyler's "I Need a Hero." If you talk the talk, then walk the walk. Put up or shut up. God is not in confusion, and he loves everybody. Things have gotten to the point where hate is engulfing America, and our leaders are making poor decisions. I feel we need relief. America is under tremendous stress these days. I can feel it in the air that this administration is filled with a wagonload of nuts—flat-out kooks. All right, let's slowly go to a place of calmness. It's all right. Things happen sometimes.

Now, can anybody remember the movie *Groundhog Day* starring Bill Murray? This movie was about waking up and reliving the same day over and over again. But something unique happened each day. He would save a little boy's life who fell from a tree. The funny thing about this incident was one day he yelled at the kid. He was inclined to say to him, "All this time I have been saving you, and you never once thanked me." The question: is it important to have your name called when you and they know who you are? I think not, but give credit to where it belongs, to God's anointed one. God gives mighty power to some of us, mostly the meek. He does it over and over again, just like *Groundhog Day*. Hope is still alive. We recognize that the stakes are high, and the parallels are drawn between Abraham Lincoln and today's Republican senators. Who rises to greatness? We are repeating history and are again aligned with President Lincoln. This part of history is being played out before our very eyes, and it's a beautiful thing. God built Americans this way for a reason, so whoever knows the reason, now is the time to step up, and may God be with you. Always remember to keep America beautiful, and never change her complexion. Our second song is Bobby Bland's "These Hands Small but Mighty."

BIGFOOT

*A*ll city folks, as well as those in the backwoods and flat-out dancing with the wolves of Alabama, I'm calling. We love you. Come on, now, and go with me to save my mule. Our song is "Ain't Too Proud to Beg" by the Temptations.

PHARISEES

his thing has plagued my mind long enough, and I feel it's time to let it out. It's about a man going on a date with Madea (Tyler Perry). Madea excites men, looking like a powerhouse gal—sort of like three or four women wrapped up in one, a back breaker. All right, let's get this date on the way. There are a few things her date needs to know. The time, place, and what Madea likes to chow down on; it's like feeding a hog with a gun. The date starts at 6:00 p.m., and it's her first feeding. It's the corner barbershop that sells food. She orders chitterlings, black-eyed peas, one pig's foot, and a Pepsi. They then proceed to go over to Cousin Neck Bone's House to dance to the oldies. At nine o'clock, she's ready to eat again, and this time it's Popeye's Chicken. She orders the family pack, which consists of twenty-five pieces. Now she's ready to dance some more, but at midnight she wants McDonald's, and it's the same order the Sexy Guy makes every Friday: eight Big Macs, three large fries, and a small Diet Coke. Don't get me wrong; I love Tyler Perry as well as Madea. I'm just working my way toward the man, the Wandering Smooch Casanova, Alabama's Backstreet Boy. Our first song is "I'm a Girl Watcher" by the O'kaysions.

All right, remember what happened when the rich man came to Jesus and asked, "What must I do to be saved?" Jesus told him to give away everything he owned and then come back. The Scriptures also explained that it's hard for a rich man to be saved because his focus is on wealth. Jesus didn't give a hoot about wealth. He cared about the people. Jesus also said, "You will know my followers by the way they treat the least." Now, God sent his son, Jesus, into the world to save people from sin. The main problem was the Pharisees. They had made themselves self-righteous people. They no longer lived by God's word and recreated the laws to suit themselves. They worshiped God as they saw fit—convenient and profitable. They were a wealthy group of people who owned land and made the laws. The Pharisees felt they were better than other people, which was a mistake Jesus had to correct. They had lost what the Scriptures taught.

This wannabe senator is a very sick individual who thinks he's above all the women accusers. These ladies are suffering, Alabama. Does anybody there really care? What's going on in Alabama? It's not God. Hold your head up, Alabama, and let this sin pass. God is not in this, and that man isn't worth any part of this evil. It's time to move away from sick people and be nicer to your womenfolk. Our song is "Praise the Lord" by Imp.

RACIST CHRISTIANS

*H*ere is the stain of racism and the so-called Christian way of life. Frank Embree was just nineteen when he was lynched. He was accused of raping a fourteen-year-old white girl. Black men accused of raping a white woman were sentenced to death by lynching in those days, which was mostly done by so-called white Christians. White Christians held the largest membership of the white race. Although this young man maintained his innocence, even after they had whipped him over one hundred times, they forced him to confess to the crime. He was hung without trial in 1899.

Maybe it's still about being white, lawless, and macho. It appears that so-called white Christians only see what they choose to see. God said in his word that when there are two or more accusers who witness the same, then come before the elders, because it's considered as the truth, which is the real Christian way. Now, that didn't happen here. Our song is Curtis Mayfield and the Impressions' "People Get Ready."

Sweet Home Mississippi

*M*y old high school football team just won the state championship again; that's three years in a row. Somebody on that team is making that block, and somebody's making the tackle. That's teamwork. Congratulations, Simmons. I send my love to Mississippi and the entire South. We have learned to live together. The country is fine. Simply concentrate on passing over this sickness, because it's deteriorating by the day and is dangerously crazy. It's 100 percent a hopeless case. Our song today is The Staple Singers' "I'll Take You There."

BACK UP, TRAIN

*S*ugar and honey is sweet and never fails to satisfy the sweet tooth. But Jesus is sweeter than the two. He surpasses all sweetness. He's the real deal, and he loves everybody, especially the most vulnerable. How sweet it is. I think America is moving away from Jesus's love and has gotten a little too funky. We are being consumed by the funk. Funkier than a group of mosquitoes, it's too much. I can't stand the funk. But wait—through it all, let's continue to love, because love never fails.

Dr. Martin Luther King wrote, "The ultimate measure of a man is not where he stands in moments of comfort and convenience, but where he stands at times of challenge and controversy." There are many of us who strive to help people and will take a stand to protect them. We are quick to recognize thieves, and God points them out because they have the wrong spirit. We will never give up to a thief, no matter the odds. The Bible states that when you have done all you can, you should still stand. I'm wondering who will stand with me; now is the time. My name has been floating around like a celebrity lately. Okay, I'm out now. Maybe I am the top cat.

It's time we work together for infrastructure, and to forget all that other tax mess because it hurts the people. It will give to the corporations and the rich—something not needed at this point in time. We can't depend on maybe something developing from the tax cut. because it's not sufficient information. That's a theory, and all this bill brings to the table is a maybe, which is definitely bad business. Now, a theory hasn't been proven. It's like saying, "I can comfortably eat a thousand hot dogs at one serving." But what we can make happen ourselves is putting together an infrastructure bill to save America with facts, not guessing, by putting our people back to work. This is the only thing that works right now. However, if a company wants to return to America, we can put in a clause that states the particular company may sign an agreement with the government, and their taxes will be reduced upon returning. No need to be guessing if they will return, because it could be US dollars lost; it's not a sure thing.

Hey, I can't do the rope pull alone; I need Democrats, Republicans, and independents. We all rock America, so let's stay together. Stop this bill. Dr. King also wrote in one of his greatest speeches, "With this faith I will go out and carve a tunnel of hope through the mountain of despair. With this faith, I will go out with you and transform dark yesterdays into bright tomorrows. With this faith, we will be able to achieve this new day when all of God's children, black men and white men, Jews and Gentiles, Protestants and Catholics, will be able to join hands and sing with the Negroes in the spiritual of old: Free at last! Free at last! Thank God almighty, we are free at last." Our main objective is to always move forward in ways that protect the people. Our song today is Otis Clay's "If I Could Reach Out."

STICK 'EM UP

*L*et's start out with a song tonight: Hall & Oates' "I Can't Go for That (No Can Do)." It never fails: every time I hear that song, I think about Magic Johnson and Larry Bird battling on the basketball court. Magic and Bird forgot about Isaiah Thomas peeping through the window—Mr. Basketball himself. Come to me, and let's sail.

It's been known for a while that the Republican leaders are egotistical morons with excessive hate toward blacks, creating out-of-control psychotic behaviors and an inappropriate emotional response projected onto the work force. These guys hate black people and have gone stone crazy, overturning every single thing that was put in place by the previous administration, which makes them sick projecting lunatics. They hate the American people for their versatility. It's evident now they hate black people. Just look at this new administration. The middle class and the poor are considered losers to them. But they're so happy romancing Donald Trump wholeheartedly—"Just loving you, baby." These guys are monsters, and they are willing to see people homeless, hungry, and sick. It's all about erasing the previous administration's accomplishments, not governing. They are so sick and filled with hate until they are willing to see America reduced to a Banana

Republic. They hate blacks that much. They think we are all stupid and continue to play the same old-fashioned race card on hateful, silly people.

Folks, we are being ripped off by desperate con men playing on your stupidity. The house and the Senate are being manipulated and showered with gifts, and in return they have to vote yes on a sick, sad bill, selling their souls. They have lost their souls to the devil, but it's not too late to stop them. Our song today is "Wake Up, Everybody" by Teddy Pendergrass, Harold Melvin & the Blue Notes.

MOVIE STAR

*D*onald Trump's tax celebration drew a group of lying cheerleaders who were flipping out. It was a mad scene straight out of hell, a quarterback sneak Tom Brady style. They all sounded like a computer that was programmed to say the same thing, or maybe a broken record. With misconceptions and huge mistakes, they couldn't have been truthfully talking about Donald Trump. He's still the creepy bogeyman who may explode any day into a fury of destruction because of his severe, extreme, psychopathic behavior. He has taken up too much of my time.

But I have come to realize something through my writings and videos: I'm ready for show business. I feel that actor inside of me trying to break out. It's like eating pop cycles riding a mule. My last post with the little boy's picture in the cotton field awakened something inside me. I remember the Mississippi cotton fields well and have decided to make a movie about it. Please don't tell me that I can't do it and can't act. I love acting, and I sing and dance in the shower. Now, I'm going to name some big-name actor, but don't worry; I might be able to hold my ground. I'm gonna get down with the get-down. Okay, I will have to be the main character, simply because I know the terrain. However, Oprah Winfrey and Morgan Freeman are from

Mississippi as well. But I'm the cotton patch boy. My wife will have to be Octavia Spencer simply because she has that timing that I understand well. Oprah has it too. But I need Oprah and Morgan Freeman as my parents. Morgan will have a problem gambling. Whoopi Goldberg will be my cousin and be married to Terrence Howard. Whoopi can't stop stealing chickens and hogs, and Terrence never tells the truth. Samuel L. Jackson and Lupita Nyong'o will also be a couple in my movie. Samuel is very violent and beats Lupita whenever he's drunk or catches her with another guy. Lupita's role is very promiscuous, and she grabs any guy available the minute Samuel turns his head, including old men. They are an endangered species when she's around. Sorry about those scenes, folks, but I know these characters well, and that's who they are; we are simply acting. These are the chosen people to play those roles. Hopefully they sign on. I think they can play those roles better than anyone else in the world.

Now, this movie will gross $500 million or more. I think I know exactly what Americans wants to see on screen. The movie will mainly focus on who did what within the Mississippi cotton fields. Contact me, Hollywood! I think I may be able to show a character on screen who has never been seen before. Our song today is Jackie Wilson's "(Your Love Keeps Lifting Me) Higher and Higher."

RIGHT TURN OR LEFT?

*A*ll right, almost all the Christians of the world celebrate December 25 as the birthday of Jesus Christ. But in actuality, it's really not Jesus's birthday. No Bible scholars know the exact month less or the date that Jesus was born. So let Donald Trump say "Merry Christmas" or whatever; it's not holy. It doesn't matter—it's just a metaphor and is not real. No one knows the exact month or date Jesus Christ was born, so come into the real world. Most of us act like kids on this date. It's all a misconception of God and his son Jesus. Because knowledge of the exact time of his birth is unknown, meaning people are tripping during this time.

That's why one needs to live every day like Christmas, because any day may be Jesus's real birthday. But please don't get me wrong; I enjoy the festivities as well. Merry, happy, or glad Christmas to all. Oh, happy holidays as well, whatever that means. All right, our song today is "Funny Christmas Fails Compilation."

COTTON FIELD

irst, I would like to thank Georgia for sharing this beautiful photo. It shows a positive outlook about dangling concepts of the cotton fields. But there is unity in this picture, and I'm rocking with you, Georgia. Now, if you think the cotton field in this day is nonessential, please take a closer look. Nothing here is dispensable; it's all good. These people aren't actually picking cotton, but I think they understand the significance of sharing the cotton field at this stage in America's history. Something good came out of that misery, and we want to see it, and I'm gonna tell the story. I'm doing it in a movie about one particular cotton field in Mississippi, and you're going to love it.

If you have been one of those people following my writings, you know that I try my best to keep it real. But there is one thing I love for sure: comedy. Comedy will be in my movie, but there is a lot more. Let's look at it like the roots of the South. Our first song is Little Milton's "We're Gonna Make It."

I'm writing my screenplay as I learn, and I'm loving it. I found that the cotton fields of Mississippi were an institution of higher learning and also a secret society. Mississippi is also the birthplace of American music. There were cool people in Mississippi long before other places. Mississippi showed the world how to be cool. What I'm actually trying to say is that one must understand and have rhythm in order to be a good cotton picker. One must be able to walk the walk and talk the talk. It's all about evolving to be a good thing. It's sort of like feeding slaves chitterlings. It turned out to be a good thing because it made them fat.

All right, back to the movie. I have read three books, gathering knowledge about Hollywood. I know now that it's a serious business, and a writer and actor needs a manager, agent, attorney, and medical doctors following him around, with a coach on the sidelines. But it's a great feeling to find another love like writing. I heard Will Smith once say that he was working while Hollywood was sleeping. Thanks, Will, for that good advice. I'm busy working like white on black—or is it black on white? Let's relax. Our song is Aretha Franklin's "Rock with Me."

PATTON'S PANTHERS

A message to the world's "smartest" human: be nice, Donald Trump. You cannot ascertain that this is *Mission Impossible*. Hey, was that you sitting between two black people, Oprah Winfrey and Don King? You might change seats now, Donald. Hey, whoops—not sustainable. They're the wrong race of people. You seem to be focused on one race, and it's the white race. I think being a genius should humble a person somewhat and teach one to have respect for God. It should also teach one sympathy for others and understanding of spiritual things. Don't act like a moron. It may also make one submissive to knowledge. But it's possible I'm wrong, because knowledge is usually hidden treasure that is better than money.

All right, let's learn, Mr. Genius. Did you know that the 761st Tank Battalion was an all-black unit that always fought up front for General Patton, your hero? They broke through enemy lines day after day in one country after another. They were usually the first to engage the enemy. They were the only unit in continuous combat for 183 days straight without relief, and their heroic actions made Patton great. They were the one group that raised the most hell in the Battle of the Bulge. In 1998, they received a Presidential Unit Citation, the highest award that a unit could receive.

They were the real badasses, just like the Red Tail Airman flyboys. The white man swept them all under the rug, making himself the hero of all, creating another period of ignorance for all Americans. Patton got all the credit, but he was actually saved by the Black Panther tankers.

Welcome to the world of reading (not Fox). Donald Trump hates people of color, and Fox is fake (aliens). Remember that a leader stands alone for the good of the people, because sometimes that's what makes him great, and it's called love for the people. I remember writing about cruising with President Obama aboard the Starship *Enterprise*. Well, let's imagine the *Enterprise* has just picked up the entire Trump Administration and is ready to take off. The question is where to, Mr. President? Donald Trump answers by saying, "Get me the hell out of here—anyplace away from the White House!" So let's go toward Jupiter. Our song today is Evelyn Champagne King's "Shame."

MOUSETRAP

*M*ost Americans these days are psychologists, because they know who's lying by the sound of one's voice. Their therapy is focused on keeping gangster behavior in check by putting soap in potty mouths. I once knew a doctor who worked alongside me. He who hypnotized his clients and got good results. Hypnosis taps into the unconscious mind and makes memory crystal clear. Everything we have learned is available for recall. The unconscious mind is basically the source that orchestrates our behavior, which includes decision-making, beliefs, and feelings.

All right, let's go to the conscious mind. It's trained to retrieve learned materials stored within the unconscious mind. It's sort of like going to the grocery store, and if your money is right, you can buy anything you want. Let's compare knowledge to money. If you have accumulated enough knowledge about your endeavor, you may be able to articulate things step by step. It's like finished homework. Now, when there is no knowledge to retrieve of the situation, or when you can't recall, it's normal for the conscious mind to immediately go into shutdown mode. There is a war going on between the unconscious mind and the conscious mind, whether its active or passive. That sometimes create noticeable problems because the mind wants to learn. God created us that way. He doesn't want us backtracking.

Here is the kicker: greater is he that is within you, than he that's in the world. God has stored things within our unconscious minds that we may come to know, and it's a *maybe*. When we pray, we are praying for God to unleash wisdom and knowledge to us, from the unconscious mind, in order to solve problems. The Bible states that one must study to learn what God approves. There's a thin line between knowledge and power, and they can both be frightening. Simply stand on knowledge and don't move. Have you ever noticed that cool people are usually level-headed and smooth? Stop and think, and then walk on the water. It's easy—just create a pair of shoes that float!

I'm wondering what have I gotten myself into with this movie thing. I'm finishing up a book and am busy with that, plus work. I have also enrolled back into college, studying acting with all the gravy. I may have enrolled in a few advanced acting classes—a simple mistake. It appears that I'm making it funky, and I can't stand myself. I want to hit the ground running and hopefully get it right. I love and believe in knowledge; it's a beautiful thing. Our song today is James Brown's "Make It Funky, Parts 1 through 4."

HITLER

et's say I have a television show. When I step out on the scene, I would surely do a sketch called "The Good Old Boy." Another name could be "Corn Bread Black Man," "Confused Black Man," or "Uncle Tom." They all mean you support Donald Trump. The key is fitting in with white evangelicals who passed over Jesus in the hopes of suppressing and controlling people of color. They are probably saying to God, "Well, Lord, you're making us lose our power, and so we decided to take it from here. We're in charge now."

It starts out with a decision made to separate the people by race with days of the week. Monday is black folks day, Tuesday is white folks day, Wednesday is Hispanics day, Thursday is Asians day, and Friday is any other race. You can use the phone, go shop, and do just about anything you like—but only on your day. There is an exception for older white males. They get all seven days of the week. It's courtesy of a racist nation designed to discriminate. That prompted me to wonder whether Hitler called himself a Christian, a godsend. I think Hitler adopted that philosophy to neutralize the Christian, and he may have been more religious than Donald Trump. But I think both these guys' theology is basically the same: it's combining their power with religion, which makes them evil. There is no difference between Donald Trump speaking at our State of the Union and Hitler speaking. They both were enemies of the state. Religion for these guys is a continual act of manipulation to keep and capture more political power through carnal Christians, at the same time instigating war and genocide, eliminating certain groups of people. It's a sick, demonic act and puts them above God.

Hitler has already carried out his demonic act of genocide, but Donald Trump is still trying to achieve his goal of genocide, and he doesn't care about any person of color. He has a heart of stone, just like Hitler. Republicans must understand the opposition before it's too late, because no one can control him. His reality is the same as Hitler's: "I want war." it's the devil himself. Our song today is Darrell Banks's "Open the Door to Your Heart."

EVERYTHING MUST CHANGE

The second amendment, which states the right to bear arms, was added in 1791. How many rounds could they shoot a minute? Now, what if people are constantly trying to invent new things that are more economical and convenient? We as humans are readjusting at a rapid pace to accommodate psychological and technological discoveries, which include guns. In all actuality, this means a change of mind. I can remember when a cell phone in the cotton fields of Mississippi was a guy riding a mule. Okay, he was called the Mule Boy, and this is how it worked.

In the cotton fields, people were usually spread out far and wide, and at times they were too far to call or see one another. That was where the mule boy was handy. All one had to do was call him and request a message be delivered to a certain person. He would stand up on the mule and locate that particular person. Then he would deliver the message as quickly as possible. Super advanced technology!

Wow, has time changed. We no longer need a mule boy and his beloved mule. We have quick communications these days with a small device called a cell phone, and it's capable of calling anyone at any place in the world. Let's imagine sending a message to Washington,

DC using a mule boy. Okay, America. We are too advanced and should no longer equate the mule boy with today's inventions. To Florida and to all-American kids, I love you. Our song today is Jerry Butler's "Ain't Understanding Mellow."

Printed in the United States
By Bookmasters